A GUIDE TO
THE ARCHITECTURE
OF WASHINGTON, D.C.

Written and edited by
Warren J. Cox,
Hugh Newell Jacobsen,
Francis D. Lethbridge,
and David R. Rosenthal
for the
Washington Metropolitan Chapter
of the
American Institute of Architects

Twenty Walking and Motoring Tours of Washington
and the Vicinity

McGRAW-HILL BOOK COMPANY
New York   St. Louis   San Francisco   Dusseldorf
London   Mexico   Sydney   Toronto

Library of Congress Card Catalogue Number:
74-1336
ISBN 0–07–013286–0
ISBN 0–07–013285–2 (pbk.)

The American Institute of Architects, the Washington
Metropolitan Chapter of the American Institute of Architects, and individuals connected with this publication
assume no legal responsibility for the completeness or
accuracy of the listings herein nor any legal responsibility
for the appreciation or depreciation in the value of any of
the premises listed herein by reason of such inclusion.

It is important to note that since houses change owners,
and owners of famous houses have a difficult time preserving privacy, owners' names have been omitted from the
listing. Note too that the listing of a house herein does not
imply that it is open to visitors. Only buildings whose description indicates visiting hours are open for inspection
without special arrangements.

ACKNOWLEDGMENT

The Editors of this second edition of *A Guide to the Architecture of Washington, D.C.,* wish to express their gratitude to Charles Atherton, Secretary of the Fine Arts Commission; Donald Canty, Editor of the *A.I.A. Journal;* and Wolf VonEckardt, architectural critic for *The Washington Post,* who acted jointly as a Board of Review to select all entries in the book which have been constructed during the past twenty-five years, thus relieving the Editors of the burden of passing judgment upon their own work and that of their contemporaries.

Thanks and appreciation are also due Heather Willson Cass, Ben Calloway Jones, and Lois H. Lenderking for their assistance in compiling and producing the Second Edition of the *Guide* and to Jane Knight, Helena Newman, Charles Egbert, and Richard Malesardi for their contributions to the first edition. The first edition, upon which the format of this edition was based, was produced by Silas Snider Associates of New York, among them editor Percy Seitlin and art director Rudi Bass—who, as representatives of the United States Steel Corporation, were responsible for editorial assistance, graphic design and production organization.

PREFACE TO THE SECOND EDITION

"Architecture is the translation of its epoch into space." —Mies van der Rohe

It was said of the first edition of this *Guide* that the buildings admitted belonged to an "exclusive club." This was true in a sense, but the "club" was, quite simply, made up of buildings which were selected exclusively because of their architectural merit or distinction, rather than historic associations, prominence or any other combination of reasons.

This book was the first compilation of significant Washington structures prepared both for the architectural profession and for those interested in the history of the city as told by its architecture. The second edition has been expanded to describe over a hundred buildings which were not in the earlier volume. There have been a few deletions because of reappraisal and others to make room for more important new entries. Of the buildings previously described, ten have been demolished during the past nine years. Of this number, the loss of the National Presbyterian Church of the Covenant at Connecticut Avenue and N Street and the Tuckerman house at 16th and I Streets were most regrettable.

The book has been arranged into walking and motoring tours, and includes an index of buildings and architects, as well as a pictorial history of the city's growth and change.

The Editors

PICTURE CREDITS

CONTENTS

THE ARCHITECTURE OF WASHINGTON, D.C. 1

STATUE OF WASHINGTON

The Architecture of Washington, D.C.

FRANCIS D. LETHBRIDGE, FAIA

The selection of a site for the Federal Capital was finally settled one evening in New York City, when Thomas Jefferson and Alexander Hamilton dined together and concluded what might be described as a political deal. Bitter political enemies though they were, in that summer of 1790 Jefferson and Hamilton each wanted something that only their combined influence in Congress could bring about. And so it came to pass that sufficient Southern votes were cast for the Funding Bill; that the Pennsylvanians, wooed by the prospect of removal to Philadelphia for the next ten years, cast their votes for the Residence Bill; and that, to the accompaniment of cries of rage from New York and New England, the Federal Government assumed the debts of the states and planned to set up its home on the shores of the Potomac River.*

View of Georgetown and the Federal City, 1801

The planning of the City of Washington is a familiar tale, yet one that bears repeating, for the quality, durability, and persistent effect of that plan upon the city must always be a central theme in the story of its architecture. We must

---

* *Journal of William Maclay,* 1789–1791 (New York, 1927). Maclay, a senator from Pennsylvania, had no illusions. His journal records (June 30, 1791): "I am fully convinced Pennsylvania could do no better. The matter could not be longer delayed. It is, in fact, the interest of the President of the United States that pushes the Potomac. He, by means of Jefferson, Madison, Carroll and others, urged the business, and if we had not closed with these terms, a bargain would have been made for the temporary residence in New York."

first, however, go somewhat further back in time, for long before the construction of the Federal City began, there was a flourishing colonial society on the shores of the Potomac near the place where the tidewater country ends. The fall line—that abrupt rise from the eastern coastal plain that marks the end of navigable water—may be traced as an uneven line from New England southward and westward. The cities of Trenton and Richmond, for example, lie at the falls of the Delaware and the James, and if the Capital had never been established on the Potomac, the ports of Georgetown and Alexandria would doubtless have prospered and grown into thriving cities by virtue of their location at this crossroads of travel by land and river.

Chesapeake Bay had been explored by the Spanish before the end of the sixteenth century, but it was not until 1608, when Captain John Smith sailed up the river, quite possibly as far as the Little Falls, north of the present site of Georgetown, that very much was known of the area that was to become the capital of the new world. Smith's *General Historie of Virginia, New England and the Summer Isles,* published in England in 1627, was accompanied by a remarkable map that was the basis for all cartography of the Chesapeake region for nearly a hundred years. His description of the river is still a vivid one:

Map of Virginia by Captain John Smith, 1607

"The fourth river is called Patawomeke, 6 or 7 myles in breadth. It is navigable 140 myles, and fed as the rest with many sweet rivers and springs, which fall from the bordering hills. These hills many of them are planted, and yeeld no lesse plentie and varietie of fruit, then the river exceedeth with abundance of fish. It is inhabited on both sides . . . The river above this place maketh his passage downe a low pleasant valley overshaddowed in many places with high rocky mountaines; from whence distill innumerable sweet and pleasant springs."

In the next twenty-five years the Potomac became a scene of increasing activity on the part of traders who began to tap a rich supply of furs, not from the adjacent country alone, but from the lands beyond the Alleghenies, from which they were carried by the Indians to the headwaters of the river. These adventurers were necessarily a hardy and resourceful lot, who plied their trade in small shallops from the lower reaches of Chesapeake Bay; and some of them, such as Henry Spelman and Henry Fleete, knew the Algonquin language well from having lived with the Indians as hostages or captives.

It was not until March, 1634 that Leonard Calvert arrived upon the Potomac with two ships, the Ark and the Dove, and a cargo of Roman Catholic settlers who were seeking fortunes as well as freedom from religious persecution. Near the mouth of the river they founded St. Mary's City, the first capital of Maryland for a brief period, of which only a few fragmentary remains exist today. There are, in fact, very few remaining examples of seventeenth century construction on either the Maryland or the Virginia shores of the river. You must travel farther south, to the banks of the James River, to the sites of the Thomas Rolfe house (1651), the Allen house, or "Bacon's Castle" (1655), and St. Luke's Church (c. 1650), to see the only recognizable survivals of Jacobean architecture in the tidewater country. It is ironic that the most famous example of the period, Governor Berkeley's mansion "Greenspring" (1642), which Waterman terms "probably the greatest Virginia house of the Century," was destroyed in 1806 to make way for B. H. Latrobe's house for William Ludwell Lee, which in its turn was demolished during the Civil War.*

Despite recurring troubles with the dwindling Indian tribes up until the beginning of the eighteenth century, settlement along the Potomac continued steadily. Large land grants were taken up in both Virginia and Maryland, and estates of many thousands of acres were not unusual. Compared to the lands of Robert Carter of Nomini Hall, who owned 63,093 acres, and William Fitzhugh of Bedford, who had acquired over 45,000 acres, the holdings of George Washington at Mount Vernon of 8,000 acres and George Mason's combined holdings along the river of about 15,000 acres seem modest in size. Cheap land, abundant labor, easy transportation from private landings to ships, and a ready market for tobacco in England made possible the development of the great plantations of the tidewater country.

View of Mount Vernon, c. 1795

---

* The Mansions of Virginia, 1706–1776. Thomas Tileston Waterman (Chapel Hill, 1946).

It was a handsome life, for the wealthier landowners, that flourished for over a hundred years and persisted for the better part of still another century. Within a relatively few miles of Washington you can see many noble examples of these country mansions of the middle and late eighteenth century,* and a short trip to Williamsburg, Virginia, will help you to imagine what life was like in a provincial capital of that period.

The prosperity of the plantations and the settlement of tracts beyond the borders of the river and its navigable tributaries stimulated the founding of the ports of Alexandria (1748) and Georgetown (1751).

Another earlier port, Garrison's Landing, known later as Bladensburg (1742), on the Eastern Branch or Anacostia River, sank into commercial obscurity at the end of the eighteenth century when the river silted up beyond that point. These Potomac ports were the scene of an important event in colonial history not long after they had been established. In the year 1755 General Braddock embarked with his army from Alexandria, landed near the foot of Rock Creek, and marched up the path of what is now Wisconsin Avenue, on the ill-fated expedition against the French and Indians that ended in disaster near Fort Duquesne. One of the few provincial officers to return unscathed from that campaign was a young Virginian who had been spared to play a greater role in history.

Georgetown and Alexandria still retain some of the atmosphere and much of the scale and texture of colonial river port towns. Most travelers seem to have agreed that by the latter part of the century they were thriving, pleasant places.

Thomas Twining, after a rough all-day wagon journey from Baltimore in 1795, described Georgetown as "a small but neat town . . . the road from Virginia and the Southern States, crossing the Potomac here, already gives an air of prosperity to this little town, and assures its future importance, whatever may be the fate of the projected metropolis." The fate of the future 'metropolis' was in fact frequently in doubt during the succeeding seventy-five years.

A stage at Bladensburg—from Isaac Weld's "Travels . . .", London, 1799

* Gunston Hall, Virginia (1753); Mount Vernon, Virginia (1757–1787); Montpelier, Laurel, Maryland (1770).

At Washington's request, the Act of 1790, specifying the location of the federal district of "ten miles square" to be located at any point *above* the Eastern Branch, was modified to include the town of Alexandria,* several miles below that point. Congress enacted this change on March 3, 1791, and by the ninth of that month Major Pierre L'Enfant had arrived in Georgetown to commence the planning of the capital city. Andrew Ellicott had already been employed to "make a Survey and Map of the Federal Territory" and they proceeded without delay to carry out as much of this work as they could before Washington's arrival at the site.

Ellicott's topographic map—from Warden's "Chorographical Description—," Paris, 1816

On the evening of March 29, a crucial meeting took place after dinner at the home of General Uriah Forrest†, at which the President, the newly appointed Commissioners, and the principal landowners of the federal district were present. The next day Washington recorded in his diary:

"The parties to whom I addressed myself yesterday evening, having taken the matter into consideration, saw the propriety of my observations; and whilst they were contending for the shadow they might lose the substance; and therefore mutually agreed and entered into articles to surrender for public purposes, one half the land they severally possessed within the bounds which were designated as necessary for the city to stand . . .

"This business being thus happily finished and some directions given to the Commissioners, the Surveyor and

---

* Alexandria was ceded back to the State of Virginia in 1846.

† This building, 3350 M Street, is still standing, mutilated by commercial alterations.

Engineer with respect to the mode of laying out the district —Surveying the grounds for the City and forming them into lots—I left Georgetown, dined in Alexandria and reached Mount Vernon in the evening."

It was only fitting that the Commissioners agreed in September "that the federal District be called 'The Territory of Columbia' and the federal City 'The City of Washington!'"

L'Enfant had less than a year to prepare the plan of the capital city before he was dismissed for his failure—or his innate inability—to acknowledge the authority of the Commissioners over his work. To the end, he maintained that he was responsible to the President alone, and when Washington himself reluctantly denied that this was so, L'Enfant's dismissal was inevitable. He had had sufficient time, nevertheless, to cast the mold in which the city had been formed, and with the sole exception of Washington himself, no man's influence upon its conception and development was greater.

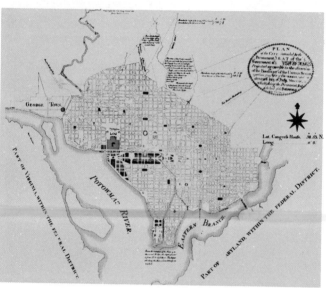

L'Enfant's plan of the City of Wasington, 1792

The architecture of the area since 1791 may be conveniently divided into four major phases. The first, which extended to the middle of the nineteenth century, is generally characterized by work in the Late Georgian and Classic Revival styles. Some designs in the Gothic Revival style were also constructed in this period, but were limited principally to small examples of ecclesiastical architecture. The second phase, in a variety of styles that might be grouped under the term Romantic Revival, was dominant from about 1850 to the end of the century. The third period, Classic Eclecticism, was to a large degree an outgrowth of the Columbian Exposition of 1893 and the McMillan Plan for Washington in 1901; and the fourth and last phase can be said to extend from about the beginning of the Second World War to the present day.

Pennsylvania Avenue, (c. 1830), looking toward the Capitol

From the first, the federal capital attracted the talents of many of the most gifted designers of the period. They included architect-builders, or "undertakers," such as William Lovering; self-taught gentleman-architects like Dr. William Thornton; and trained professional architect-engineers, of whom Benjamin Henry Latrobe was the most notable example. Some, like James Hoban, architect of the White House, and Charles Bulfinch, who succeeded Latrobe as architect of the Capitol in 1818, do not fit neatly into any of these categories.

In an era that was not distinguished by temperance of speech and writing in the political arena, architects frequently indulged in bitter personal invective. Architects have been inclined to disagree with one another since the beginning of time and will probably continue to do so until the end, but they have seldom expressed themselves so forcefully in writing as in the case of:

(a) Thornton vs. Latrobe:

"This Dutchman in taste, this monument builder,
This planner of grand steps and walls,
This falling-arch maker, this blunder-roof gilder,
Himself still an architect calls."

(b) Latrobe vs. Hoban:

". . . the style he [Jefferson] proposes is exactly consistent with Hoban's pile—a litter of pigs worthy of the great sow it surrounds, and of the wild Irish boar, the father of her . . ."

(c) Hadfield vs. Thornton, et al:

"This premium [for the best design of the Capitol] was offered at a period when scarcely a professional architect was to be found in any of the United States; which is plainly to be seen in the pile of trash presented as designs for said building."

Paradoxically, these men who hurled such violent criticism at one another lived in an age of harmonious urban architecture, for despite personal animosities and professional jealousies, they were all working within the limits of generally accepted standards of taste, and perhaps just as importantly, within fairly narrow limits of available construction materials and techniques.*

View of the City of Washington from beyond the Navy Yard. c. 1834

Although construction of the first major public buildings, the White House and the Capitol, had begun in 1793—seven years before the government moved to Washington —they were virtually rebuilt anew after the sack and burning of the Capital by British troops in 1814. The rout of the hastily assembled militia at the Battle of Bladensburg (known thereafter as "The Bladensburg Races") caused President Madison, Madame Madison, and the rest of official Washington to beat a hasty retreat to the suburbs. The President returned to take up temporary residence in Col. John Tayloe's town house, the Octagon (now national headquarters of the American Institute of Architects); and the Treaty of Ghent, which ended the War of 1812, was signed in the round room on the second floor of that historic house.

In the early eighteen-thirties the commercial future of the city was thought to lie in the hoped-for success of the Chesapeake and Ohio Canal which was being constructed between Washington and Cumberland, Maryland, to connect the Potomac with the headwaters of the Ohio River. The canal was completed, and continued in operation until 1923, but it was never a profitable investment, because the Baltimore and Ohio Railroad, following much the same route with its eastern terminus at Baltimore, had been begun at exactly the same time (and this with remarkable optimism, since a successful steam locomotive had not

---

* See, for example, Thornton's "Tudor Place," and the Octagon; Latrobe's Decatur House and St. John's Church, Lafayette Square; The White House—central facade by Hoban and Latrobe; and Hadfield's Arlington House and Old City Hall.

yet been invented). The canal today is a valuable recreational area—an attractive stretch for hiking, cycling, and canoeing.*

George Hadfield's City Hall, c. 1840

When Robert Mills was Architect of Public Buildings in 1841, he supplemented his modest income by producing a *Guide to the National Executive Offices and the Capitol of the United States,* a slim paperbound volume of only fifty pages—which is chiefly curious today because within those covers he was able to include plans of the Capitol and of all the executive buildings, to list the names and room numbers of all federal employes, and to have room left over to print the menu for the Congressional Dining Room or "Refectory for Members of Congress."†

Mills, who had been a pupil of Latrobe, Ammi Young, and Thomas U. Walter were probably the last federal architects of the period to design work in the Classic Revival style. In 1849 a book was published, *Hints on Public Architecture,* by Robert Dale Owen, the son of Robert Owen, leader of the utopian colony of New Harmony. The younger Owen, a former representative from Indiana, was Chairman of the Building Committee of the Smithsonian Institution, and his book is an elaborate presentation of, and argument for, the honest functional qualities of James Renwick's design, "exemplifying the style of the twelfth century" as contrasted with the false qualities of the Greek and Roman manner of other public buildings in Washington. The book and the design appear to have been strongly influenced by the writings of A. Welby Pugin and Andrew Jackson Downing, and some of the text gives one the impression that though time may pass and styles may change, architectural jargon remains usable for any occasion:

---

*Barge trips are conducted by the Park Service during the summer months from the lock at the foot of Thirtieth Street in Georgetown.

†Some of the fixed prices were: venison steak, 37½¢; beefsteak, 25¢; pork steak, 25¢; mutton chop, 25¢; veal cutlet, 25¢; one dozen raw oysters, 12½¢; ham and eggs 37½¢; one plate of common turtle soup, 25¢; one plate of green turtle soup, 50¢; wine and water, and malt liquor, per tumbler, 6¼¢.

Renwick's design for the Smithsonian Institution. 1849

". . . to reach an Architecture suited to our own coumtry and our own time . . . an actual example, at the Seat of Government, the architect of which seems to me to have struck into the right road, to have made a step in advance, and to have given us, in his design, not a little of what may be fitting and appropriate in any manner . . . that shall deserve to be named as a National Style of Architecture for America."

Not many architects chose to follow Renwick's new "National Style" (Renwick himself, when he designed the old Corcoran Gallery some years later, adopted the style of the French Renaissance), but most architects thereafter seemed determined to submit their own candidates for that honor.

Before his death in a Hudson riverboat explosion; Downing had laid out the grounds of the Smithsonian and the White House in the romantic, meandering style of the period. His popular books on landscape design and rural architecture publicized residential designs by A. J. Davis, Richard Upjohn, and Downing's own partner, Calvert Vaux, who planned houses for some of the fashionable and wealthy citizens of Georgetown over a number of years—houses that show, in an interesting way, the transition of residential design from the late Classic Revival through the relatively chaste Italianate or "Tuscan Villa" style to the heavily ornamented, mansard-roofed houses of the latter part of the nineteenth century.

"Residence of the Author," Downing's "Landscape Gardening and Rural Architecture," N.Y. 1849

The Civil War turned the City of Washington into an armed camp. The location of the Capital, selected so carefully to be near the line between the North and South became a position at the edge of the battlefront. A ring of defensive forts was constructed on the hills surrounding the city, and although a Confederate army led by Jubal Early reached the outskirts of the District at Fort Stevens, the city's defenses were never penetrated.*

Civil War Encampment on the northern outskirts of the city, 1864

Apart from the completion of the new Capitol wings and dome, work on which continued despite the war, there was comparatively little construction of a permanent nature going on in the city until the end of hostilities. A significant aftermath, however, was increased influence and activity on the part of the Army Corps of Engineers—not restricted to works of engineering alone, but extending to the design or supervision of construction of major public buildings such as the Pension Building and the old State, War and Navy Building. Most prominent in the Corps at that time was General Montgomery Meigs, the talented Army officer who had earlier challenged Thomas U. Walter's authority as Architect of the Capitol. Meigs is credited with the design of the astonishing post-Civil War Pension Building, but left what may be his most enduring monument in the Washington aqueduct system, extending to the city from above the Little Falls of the Potomac. Two of the bridges along its route are especially notable—the Cabin John Aqueduct Bridge, which for many years was the longest stone arch in the world (220 feet), and the Rock Creek Aqueduct Bridge, where the road was carried on the arched tubular metal pipes of the water supply system.

---

* See Barnard, *Defenses of Washington* (Wash., 1871). The remains of this chain of earthwork defenses are now under the jurisdiction of the Park Service. Fort Stevens, at the head of Georgia Avenue, N.W., is probably the most interesting historically, if not topographically.

State, War and Navy Building, c. 1885

The construction of the old State, War and Navy Building after the Civil War was considered by many to be an act signifying the permanence of Washington, D. C. as the site of the national capital, and if cost of construction and permanence of materials are any measure of that intent, it must have served admirably to make the intention clear. Alfred B. Mullet was not an architect whose work rests lightly upon the earth (the Post Office Building in St. Louis is another good example of his work). Like MacArthur's Philadelphia City Hall, his buildings are as much an expression of civic confidence as of architectural diligence.

The Arts and Industries Building, Smithsonian Institution, c. 1885

The Smithsonian's Arts and Industries Building, designed by Cluss and Shulze, is an interesting survival from the exhibition architecture of the 1875 Philadelphia Centennial Exposition. The oriental flavor of its form and polychrome decorations was echoed in some of the city's market buildings, schools, railroad stations, and residences of the eighteen-eighties, of which relatively few remain. The influence of H. H. Richardson and of the Romanesque Revival made an impression on Washington architecture from about 1880 to 1900, and although Richardson's Hay and Adams houses were destroyed to build the hotel that bears their names, the Tuckerman House, built the year of his death on an adjoining site, was carried out by Hornblower and Marshall in a direct continuity of style and exterior detailing. The Presbyterian Church of the Covenant, designed by J. C. Cady, architect of the Museum of Natural History in New York, and the Old Post Office on Pennsylvania Avenue, are other important examples of the period.*

Post Office, Pennsylvania Avenue, c. 1920, before construction of the Federal Triangle. The Raleigh Hotel, now demolished, is in the background.

The Washington, D.C. firm of Smithmeyer and Pelz was prominent on the architectural scene toward the end of the nineteenth century, with buildings to its credit as widely different as Georgetown's Healy Hall, a Victorian neo-Gothic college building, and the Library of Congress, a competition-winning design in the Renaissance style. Some of the more startling designs of this versatile firm were never built, including a Gothic multi-towered bridge across the Potomac, a new White House spanning 16th Street at Meridian Hill, and Franklin Smith's proposal for the "Halls of the Ancients," a sort of permanent world's fair of architecture that would have extended from the west side of the Ellipse to the river.

The lack of any effective controls over its rapid and haphazard growth was gradually destroying any evidence of a capital as a uniquely planned city, but in the year 1901 the American Institute of Architects played a central role in the initiation of the McMillan Plan, which modified, enlarged, and reestablished L'Enfant's plan of Washington. Glenn Brown, an architect whose deep interest in the history of the Capitol later produced a monumental two-volume account of its development, had been appointed Secretary of the Institute in 1899, and it was largely through his efforts that the program for the A.I.A. convention of 1900

---

* Of these three buildings, only the old Franklin Post Office still remains (1974), the others having been demolished in the late 1960's to make way for new speculative office buildings.

was prepared. The convention was held in Washington on the centennial of the establishment of the Federal City, and the papers delivered at that meeting inspired Senator McMillan, Chairman of the Senate District Committee, to appoint a commission to study the planning of the city. He asked the Institute to suggest the names of men most qualified to serve, and by common consent the names of Daniel H. Burnham and Frederick Law Olmsted, Jr., were proposed. The Chicago Columbian Exposition was still fresh in the minds of all, and Burnham, having headed the group of architects and artists who planned that exhibition, was a logical choice, as was Olmsted, son and successor of the famous landscape architect who had designed the grounds and terraces of the Capitol. Burnham and Olmsted, in turn, asked for the appointment of architect Charles Follen McKim and sculptor Augustus St. Gaudens, both of whom had worked intimately with Burnham during the Columbian Exposition in 1893. The Report of the Park Commission,

The Court of Honor, Columbian Exposition, 1893

Drawing of the 1901 Park Commission design plan for The Mall.

published in 1902, was a remarkable document, since the small group of talented men, bound together by bonds of friendship, respect and common purpose, made the most of this opportunity to describe and delineate a vision of what the city might become.

Some of the Park Commission's recommendations were never carried out—among them ideas that could be profitably restudied today—but many of them were, and the effect upon Washington's architectural style was just as pronounced as the effect upon its plan. The formality of L'Enfant's plan was restored, and the argument that an architecture derived from classical antecedents was the only suitable style for such a plan was persuasively presented, in visual terms. Whatever weight or merit this argument may have had, it is undeniably true that some of the finest buildings in Washington date from the early decades of this century quite simply because the best architects in the country designed them.

It was a time of great optimism, clients wanted and would pay for the best, and Art was respectable enough to sit at the table when the money was being served. Not only were Burnham; McKim, Mead and White; Henry Bacon; Paul Cret; Cass Gilbert, and other prominent architects of the period given important commissions in the capital, but their buildings were embellished by the work of sculptors such as St. Gaudens, Daniel Chester French, and Lorado Taft.

The spirit that pervaded the best work of that period seems gradually to have been lost. Whether it was dried up by the depression, squeezed out by the weight of bureaucracy, or simply enfeebled by lack of conviction and talent would be hard to say. Whatever the cause, work in the style of Academic Classicism, with few exceptions, seemed to become progressively larger, more sterile, and less graceful in conception and execution.

Model of first-prize design by Eliel and Eero Saarinen, R. F. Swanson, Associate, for the Smithsonian Gallery of Art, 1939

It is difficult to view architecture in Washington since 1940 in any clear historical perspective. Dating a new phase of architectural development from a period at the beginning of World War II is in itself a somewhat arbitrary decision, but the Saarinen competition-winning design for the Smithsonian Gallery of Art in 1939 (which was never constructed), and William Lescaze's Longfellow Building, in 1940, probably mark as distinct a point of change as any that might be named. Since that time, certain other isolated examples such as the Dulles Airport Terminal building loom up as important and serious works of architecture, but there has been a leveling influence of sorts at work. The majority of contemporary commercial office buildings and governmental office buildings have tended to become larger and more standardized to the point where they are virtually indistinguishable in form. This is perhaps inevitable since the functions of these structures are very nearly the same. The great variety of industrially produced materials and building components that have become available during the past thirty-five years, and the economies of modern curtain wall construction have created a new element in the cityscape that is both monotonous and distracting: monotonous, because many of the newer buildings are wrapped, like packages, in an overall pattern of windows and spandrels; distracting, because there seems to be no limit to the number of unsuitable patterns that can be placed in juxtaposition to one another.

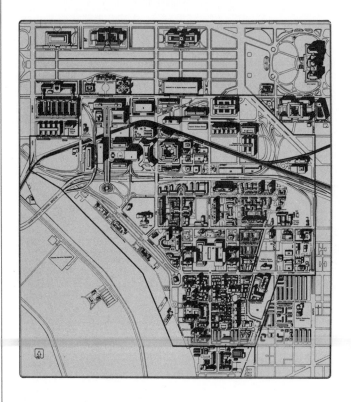

Southwest Washington Redevelopment Plan, c 1969

Washington is a horizontal city. The maximum building heights established by Congress in 1901, to prevent our principal federal monuments from being overshadowed by commercial construction, are in general still considered to be a desirable limitation, but these height limits, coupled with building programs calling for hundred of thousands of square feet of construction, have created architectural and planning problems within the city that are still unresolved.

The urban renewal area in Southwest Washington will probably remain interesting to architects and planners for many years, not only as the first large-scale application of the powers of urban renewal but also as an architectural sampler of the mid-twentieth century; for it is unusual to be able to view such a variety of architectural solutions to essentially the same problem, constructed in such a relatively concentrated area, over such a short period of time.

There are also some exceptional examples of planned communities near Washington that are of particular interest, ranging from Greenbelt, Maryland, the most famous of the government-sponsored resettlement housing projects of the nineteen-thirties, and Hollin Hills in Virginia, a pioneer example of postwar contemporary development planning, to Reston, conceived as a New Town, which is now taking form in nearby Fairfax County.

The Pennsylvania Avenue Plan, an artist's sketch from the Treasury terrace. c 1964

POSTSCRIPT, 1964–1974

The past decade has seen significant changes in the expectations, attitudes and demands of the people of the city, both black and white. The riots of 1968, Resurrection City and the outpouring of young demonstrators against the Vietnam War were dramatic evidences of change, but there have been less dramatic changes which are just as important to the architectural and topographical future of the city. There has been growing concern for the preservation of older buildings and places within the city which contribute to its cultural vitality and variety. There has been growing disenchantment with the wholesale demolition which has accompanied, and the overbearing scale which has characterized so much of the Federal city planning and reconstruction process. Resistance to the construction of more freeways within the city, organized opposition on the part of communities within the city to overly permissive zoning and, on a smaller scale, the struggle to save the old Post Office on Pennsylvania Avenue all reflect changing beliefs of what constitutes progress—all question the sanity of any planning which fails to sustain and to encourage the humane qualities of the city which make life within it bearable.

Plans for the reconstruction of Pennsylvania Avenue are a good case in point. It may be that the initial plans which were unveiled in 1964, sweeping away all of the existing buildings on the north side of the Avenue from the Treasury to the Capitol and retaining only the tower of the Post Office as a relic of the nineteenth century on the south side, will follow the same course as did earlier plans of the government to "Federalize" Lafayette Square. Those plans were ultimately supplanted by a less drastic reconstruction which was actually carried out, preserving the residential scale of the east and west sides of the Square. The Pennsylvania Avenue Plan is now being restudied and modified with the avowed intention of saving some of the fine older buildings which were formerly slated for demolition and with the aim of bringing more mixed commercial and residential uses into the area. It is well that the planners have had a chance to reconsider, for now that the F.B.I. Building has been constructed (as the first block to conform to the earlier plan, but without the arcaded street facade recommended by the Commission) a vision of the north side of the Avenue filled with a succession of such buildings was enough to cool one's enthusiasm for whatever noble qualities it may have embodied. To the credit of Nathaniel Owings and others who have been active in the planning process, they have remained receptive to changing needs and conditions in their efforts to move this important project ahead.

From the Rayburn Building, to the Kennedy Center, to the F.B.I. Building, and now to the proposed Eisenhower Convention Center, the planning and architectural problems of dealing with such immense, relatively low buildings within the city appear to be virtually insurmountable. During the past ten years the area south of Independence Avenue, as it parallels the Mall, has been filled with new Federal Office Buildings, just as monumental and just as lifeless as the Federal Triangle of the nineteen-twenties, but lacking the unity of concept and style wich were present in that undertaking. The Mall has become the site of a new group of buildings for the Smithsonian Institution, buildings which share only the general discipline of their location. Fortunately, the scale of the great central lawn, with its flanking panels of trees, is so vast that aberrations of form are visually submerged with scarcely a ripple.

If the work of any architect during the past decade is to be singled out for its contribution to the city, one must note I. M. Pei's Christian Science Church at 16th and I Streets and office buildings at L'Enfant Plaza. Both stand well above the level of quality of similar buildings of the period in their maturity of concept and execution. The new addition to the National Gallery (now under construction on the Mall), by the same architect, promises to be one of the Capitol's most original and exciting structures—complex but complete in its logic and form.

In 1967 President Johnson requested the development of a new "racially and economically balanced community" on one of the largest single undeveloped sites still remaining within the District of Columbia. Fort Lincoln New Town, to be built on the grounds of the former National Training School for Boys was conceived as an urban community, a prototype for other Federally sponsored new-towns-within-town, and a laboratory for innovative social, ecological and educational planning. With a change in administration the project never received the support that had been originally envisioned and although it has continued to progress slowly in a modified form, under the aegis of private developers, its ultimate disposition is still in doubt.

The Georgetown Waterfront. Reconstruction proposed by the Georgetown Planning Group.

Mushrooming new construction in Rosslyn, just across the river from the old port of Georgetown, and in Crystal City, an office and residential complex close to the National Airport, have transformed parts of the nearby Virginia skyline into what has been called Houston-on-the-Potomac. The Georgetown waterfront, long depressed by anachronistic industrial zoning and by the blighting influence of an unattractive elevated freeway, has begun to stir to the sound of new construction, and an effort is being made to reconcile opportunities for residential and commercial development, on what is potentially one of the most advantageous sites in the city, with the need to preserve the valuable historic buildings and enclaves that enrich the area.

And last, one must mention "Metro," of which there is much evidence throughout the city. The Washington Metropolitan Area Transit Authority has undertaken one of the most extensive, and expensive, public works projects in history, amounting to over three billion dollars of construction. The architectural design of the system has been under the direction of Harry Weese Associates, with DeLeuw Cather and Company acting as general engineering consultants. The subway, with rail extensions reaching far out into Maryland and Virginia, will unquestionably have a profound influence upon the form of future development of the city and its suburbs. Until that time, we can grit our teeth and hope that someday the streets will be repaved again.

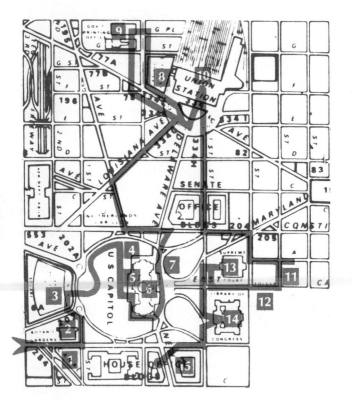

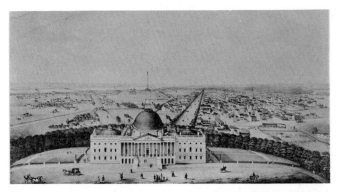

The impact of the great Dome and the Plaza dominates even the most monumental of the city's buildings. It is felt everywhere—from the most impressive structures to the low-scale residential side streets.

Lined with arching elms, L'Enfant's great avenues radiate from the Plaza and reach into the quadrants of the city, so that the Dome is visible from their respective axes.

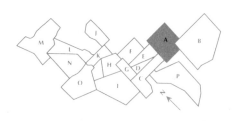

1

BARTHOLDI FOUNTAIN
2nd and B Streets, S.W.
1876—A. Bartholdi

2

BOTANIC GARDENS
1st and 2nd Streets; B Street and Maryland Avenue
1902—Bennett, Parsons and Frost
HOURS: 9 A.M. TO 4 P.M., WEEKDAYS
9 A.M. TO 12, SATURDAYS
ADMISSION FREE

Although the Mall side of the Gardens is in keeping with its neighbors of that era, the large glazed archways of the entrance and the glass-domed rotunda behind are direct responses to the problem of moving and growing full-size trees. The present building is the replacement for various temporary shelters which housed the botanical spoils of various 19th-century expeditions.

3

GRANT MEMORIAL
1st Street and East Mall
1922—Pedestal: E. P. Casey
      Statuary: Henry Shrady

Some 252 feet in length, this is the largest and most expensive statuary grouping in the city. General Grant on horseback is an equestrian statue second only in size to that of Victor Emmanuel in Rome.

4

SPRING GROTTO
1874–1875—F. L. Olmsted

This "cool retreat" for hot summer days was built as part of Olmsted's general landscaping. The Grotto now flows with city water; the original spring turned impure and had to be diverted.

5

THE CAPITOL—WEST TERRACE
(Bear right up the steps)
1874–1875—F. L. Olmsted

6a

William Thornton's winning design for the Capitol.

THE CAPITOL
1793–1802—William Thornton
1803–1817—Benjamin Henry Latrobe
1819–1829—Charles Bulfinch
1836–1851—Robert Mills
1851–1865—Thomas Ustick Walter
HOURS: 9 A.M. TO 4 P.M. DAILY

"... the first temple dedicated to the sovereignty of the
people embellishing with Athenian taste the course of a
nation looking far beyond the range of Athenian destinies."
—Thomas Jefferson to Benjamin H. Latrobe, 1812

1791—After examining the new Federal District, Pierre
Charles L'Enfant reported that he "... could discover no
one [situation] so advantageously to greet the congressional
building as that on the west end of Jenkins heights ..."
Near the center of the city-to-be, and some 88 feet above
the Potomac, Jenkins Hill, he believed, was "... a pedestal
waiting for a monument ..."

6b

Watercolor by Benjamin H. Latrobe made prior to the War of 1812.

1792—Competitions were held for the design of the Capitol and President's House. The newspaper notice announcing that for the Capitol read:

"A premium of a lot in the city of Washington . . . and $500 shall be given by the Commissioners of the Federal Buildings to the person who before the 15th of July, 1792, shall produce to them the most approved plan for a Capitol to be executed in this city."

Dr. William Thornton was allowed to submit his winning design three months after the official deadline; the officials had been reluctant to pick one of the sixteen other entries. General Washington recommended the Thornton design immediately:

"The grandeur, the simplicity, and the beauty . . . will, I doubt not, give it a preference in your eyes as it has in mine."

1793—On September 18, George Washington laid the cornerstone of the Capitol, and construction began under the supervision of Stephen Hallet, runner-up in the competition. Thornton, a doctor, was himself unqualified to construct the building. Hallet soon inserted so many of his own ideas that James Hoban, winner of the competition for the President's House, was put in charge, with Hallet as his assistant. Under their guidance, the North Wing was completed. Congress met in Washington for the first time in November 1800.

1803—Benjamin Henry Latrobe, appointed Surveyor of Public Buildings by Jefferson, took over construction of the Capitol. By 1807, he had completed the South Wing and had begun repairs and alterations to the North Wing.

1814—Admiral Cockburn of the British Navy set fire to "this harbor of Yankee democracy" on August 24. After the war, Congress moved into a temporary "Brick Capitol" on the site of the present Supreme Court, and Latrobe began reconstruction of what he called ". . . a most magnificent ruin."

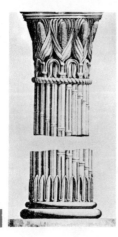

Latrobe's corncob capital.

1817—Latrobe resigned under pressure; having restored the House and Senate chambers and developed his corn-cob and tobacco-leaf capitals. Latrobe wrote to Jefferson that he had "more applause from members of Congress . . ." because of these capitals "than all the Works of Magnitude that surrounded them."

Although the exterior work during Latrobe's tenure closely followed Thornton's original design, the rooms within are by Latrobe's hand.

The famous fued between Latrobe and Thornton grew out of their disputes over the construction and execution of the Capitol. But it was Jefferson who summed up Latrobe's contribution. He wrote Latrobe:

"I declared on many and all occasions that I considered you as the only person in the United States who could have executed the . . . [House] Chamber . . ."

View of the Capitol after Bulfinch's alteration was completed c. 1830.

1827—Under Charles Bulfinch, Latrobe's successor, the link between the two wings was completed and domed, closely following Thornton's original design. Bulfinch was also responsible for improving the grounds and adding steps, terraces, the gate house, and fences.

Thomas U. Walter's elevation drawing of the Capitol.

1850—Congress authorized a competition for the design of two extensions. Thomas Ustick Walter, whose scheme included replacing the dome with a larger one, was chosen as winner.

1857—The House extension was completed and occupied.

1859—The Senate extension was completed and occupied.

Photograph taken during construction of Capitol Dome and Wings c. 1862.

1863—On December 2, Thomas Crawford's statue of Freedom was placed atop the dome. This dome—two trussed shells of cast iron, one superimposed on the other—springs from a drum whose design is based on that of St. Peter's in Rome. The dome rises 285 feet above the eastern plaza. Legend has it that the 36 columns of the drum represent the number of states and that the 13 columns of the lantern stand for the original colonies. However, there were only 34 states in 1862, and there are actually only 12 columns in the lantern. All of the trim, cornices, and columns are cast iron painted to resemble marble.

The completed Capitol after the erection of the Dome and House and Senate Wings by Walter, c. 1866.

Lincoln had continued the construction of the Capitol during the war because he believed that:

"If people see the Capitol going on . . . it is a sign we intend the Union shall go on."

Minor functional renovations followed before the end of the century:

1865—Steam heating

1874—Elevators

1881—Fireproofing

1882—A modern drainage system

1959–60—Under the direction of J. George Stewart, Architect of the Capitol, the East Front of the Capitol was extended outwards 32½ feet. This controversial change added some 102 rooms and provided a visually deeper base for the dome. The stonework was changed from sandstone to marble in the process. It is worth noting that such an extension had been proposed by Thomas U. Walter.

1966–74—A proposal to redesign and extend the West Front of the Capitol aroused a new storm of controversy which is, as yet, unresolved. An engineering report, prepared by consultants Praeger, Kavanagh and Waterbury in 1970, refuted Stewart's contention that such an extension was necessary for structural reasons and sustained the view that restoration of the West Front was feasible.

George Malcolm White succeeded J. George Stewart as architect of the Capitol upon the latter's death in 1970.

LAMPSTAND

WAITING STATION
c. 1875—F. L. Olmsted

These stations were knows as "Herdics" after the Herdic Phaeton Co., whose line of horse-drawn, yellow plush upholstered trolleys they served.

CITY POST OFFICE
Massachusetts Avenue and North Capitol
1914—Graham and Burnham

With its central Ionic colonnade and slightly projecting entrance pavilions, this building is properly in harmony with, but subordinate to, Union Station.

GOVERNMENT PRINTING OFFICE
North Capitol between G and H Streets, N.W.
1861

This massive block contains the world's largest printing establishment.

10

UNION STATION AND PLAZA
The Intersection of Massachusetts
and Louisiana Avenues, N.W.
1908—Daniel H. Burnham

COLUMBUS MEMORIAL FOUNTAIN
1908—Lorado Taft

"The frequent occurrence of the arch is always delightful in distant effect, partly on account of its graceful line, partly because the shade it casts is varied in depth, becoming deeper and deeper as the grotto retires, and partly because it gives great apparent elevation to the walls it supports."

—John Ruskin, *The Poetry of Architecture*, 1873

This was the first building to be inspired by the McMillan Commission—Roman Beaux-Arts, direct from the Columbian Exposition of 1893 in Chicago. The entrance loggia, the main waiting room, and the concourse, however, are among Washington's truly monumental interior spaces.

By the Bicentennial, they will be converted to the National Visitor Center, with parking and a new railway terminal behind.

11

MUSEUM OF AFRICAN ARTS
(Frederick Douglass townhouse)
316–318 A Street, N.E.
1870
1971—Robert Nash Associates, restoration and addition
HOURS: 11 A.M. TO 5 P.M., WEEKDAYS
         12:30 P.M. TO 5 P.M. WEEKENDS

This was the first Washington home to be occupied by Frederick Douglass, ex-slave, American statesman and editor of an abolitionist weekly paper.

FOLGER SHAKESPEARE LIBRARY
201 East Capitol Street, S.E.
1932—Paul P. Cret and Alexander B. Trowbridge,
consulting architect.
HOURS: 11 A.M. TO 4:30 P.M. MONDAY–SATURDAY

Nineteen thirties "governmental modern" without; Elizabethan (including a theatre) within. The elevations are, however, a serious attempt to be in sympathy with the surroundings without resorting to historicism.

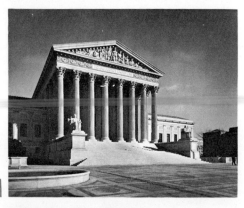

SUPREME COURT BUILDING
1st and East Capitol Streets, N.E.
1935—Cass Gilbert
HOURS: 9 A.M. TO 4:30 P.M., WEEKDAYS
9 A.M. TO 12 SATURDAYS; CLOSED SUNDAYS

"In matters of grave importance, style, not sincerity, is the vital thing . . ."
—Oscar Wilde, *The Importance of Being Earnest*
This is one of Washington's last major examples of academic classicism. Only the Archives and the Lincoln Memorial, its two near contemporaries in that waning school, can approach the massive scale and official grandeur. The relative austerity of the flanking wings is an attempt to harmonize with the neighboring Folger library.

14

LIBRARY OF CONGRESS
1st and Independence Avenue, S.E.
1886–1897—Smithmeyer and Pelz
HOURS: 9 A.M. TO 10 P.M. WEEKDAYS
        9 A.M. TO 6 P.M. SATURDAYS
        2 P.M. TO 6 P.M. SUNDAYS

"That false idea of grandeur which consists mainly in hoisting a building up from a reasonable level of the ground, mainly in order to secure for it a monstrous flight of steps which must be surmounted before the main door can be reached . . ."

—Russell Sturgis, on the main entrance, 1898

Thomas Jefferson maintained that "there is no subject to which a Member of Congress may not have occasion to refer." To replace the volumes consumed in the burning of the Capitol in 1814, Jefferson sold his great private library to the government at cost. From this core the Library of Congress has grown into the largest and best equipped library in the world. The building is based on the Paris Opera House, and the interiors, particularly the central stair hall, are accordingly heroic and florid. In the main reading room, however, the opening of a book becomes a noble rite.

15

OLD HOUSE OFFICE BUILDING
New Jersey and Independence Avenues, S.E.
1908—Carrère and Hastings

Nonidentical twins flanking the Capitol, the commission for the Senate and House Office was divided by the two architects: Hastings was responsible for the House Office Building; Carrère, for the Senate. These are properly subdued "background" buildings for the Capitol.

As the new city began to grow, it spread into the southeast quadrant before once and for all shifting back to the northwest. Houses, many of them once occupied by senators and representatives (some of them still are), as well as a church by Latrobe (where there is a list of famous parishioners), are inland. When the Navy Yard and the Congressional Cemetery were established, the Anacostia River was navigable to Bladensburg, Maryland. This is now one of the city's forgotten areas. Bypassed by most people, it deserves better treatment.

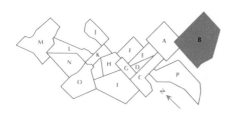

1

THE NAVY YARD
8th and M Streets, S.E.
Entrance Gate
1804—Benjamin H. Latrobe

In 1800, this was one of six such Navy yards on the East coast. Although little more than the entrance gate remains of his work here, and it has been heavily altered, Latrobe did the first planning and buildings. It is notable now not only for the magnificent Victorian officers' houses but also for the seemingly endless "Functional Tradition" factories and warehouses.

1

THE NAVY YARD
COMMANDANT'S HOUSE
(Tingey House)
1805—Sometimes attributed to Benjamin H. Latrobe

2

MARINE BARRACKS AND COMMANDANT'S HOUSE
8th and I Streets, S.E.
1805—George Hadfield
1901—Additions, Hornblower and Marshall

Framed by the simple arcaded brick barracks and with the drill field for a mall, the Commandant's House is the focal point here. It is the only building of the original group still standing.

3

SIMMONS HOUSE
314–316 9th Street, S.E.
1967—Thomas B. Simmons

One of the few contemporary houses in an area otherwise restored and reproduced. The cutaway roof is a tool to exploit the full, private use of the site.

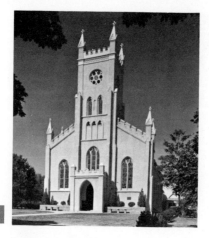

4

CHRIST CHURCH
620 G Street, S.E.
1805—Original by Benjamin H. Latrobe, but now altered

This charming and apparently naive little building was not only the frequent church of Presidents Madison, Jefferson and J. Q. Adams, but also was one of the first Gothic Revival buildings in this country.

5

THE MAPLES
(Friendship House Settlement)
630 South Carolina Avenue, S.E.
1795—William Lovering, architect-builder

". . . this fine house in the woods between Capitol Hill and the Navy Yard," as George Washington is said to have described it, has now had a city grow up around it. In spite of this, the addition of wings, and a succession of different occupants—including a hospital—the house has lost little of its character or utility.

6

SAINT MARK'S CHURCH
3rd and A Streets, S.E.
1888–1894 — T. Buckler Chequier

Here Romanesque Revival elements combine with a more Gothic Revival format. The structure is completely exposed inside and out: layered brick, timber roofing and cast-iron columns.

That this church survives at all is a tribute to one of the most alive and well congregations in the city.

7

BROWN-SPANGLER HOUSE
120 4th Street, S.E.
c. 1867
Restoration, 1958–1968 — C. Dudley Brown

A meticulous restoration of a fine post–Civil War townhouse. Brownstone steps, cast iron and a bracketed wood cornice give the exterior facade distinction. Within are the marble mantels, ornate plasterwork and high ceilings which grace the more pretentious houses of the period.

EASTERN MARKET
7th and C Streets, S.E.
1871—Adolph Cluss

This is the only remaining one of several such brick markets in the city that is still in active use as an old-fashioned meat, fish and produce market. Both inside and outside it is a refreshing change from standardized, sanitized and depersonalized supermarkets.

PHILADELPHIA ROW
120–152 Eleventh Street, S.W.
1856—George Gessford

Southwest's counterpart to Cox's Row and Smith's Row in Georgetown, somewhat smaller in scale and, more curiously, forty years later. The cornice is Victorian, but the style is still Greek Revival.

POTOMAC GARDENS APARTMENTS
1225 G Street, S.E.
1967—Metcalf and Associates

There are 352 low-rent apartments in 14 buildings; 144 of the units were designed especially for the elderly. The project includes recreational, administrative and geriatric facilities.

CONGRESSIONAL CEMETERY
18th and E Streets, S.E.
1807

Although once the semiofficial Congressional burial ground, Architects Thornton, Hadfield, and Mills lie here among the senators and congressmen. Many of the latter are commemorated by the official cenotaphs designed by Latrobe.

Senator Hoar of Massachusetts remarked on the floor of the Senate that being interred beneath one of these monuments added a new terror to death.

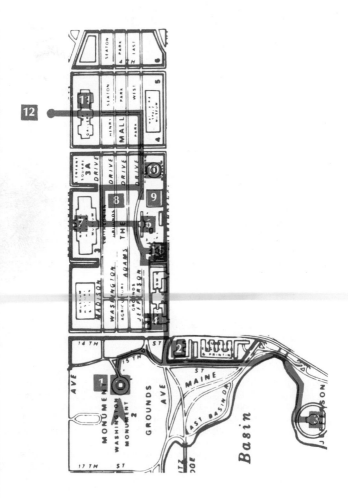

Robert Mills' competition-winning design for the Washington Monument.

The Mall is the oldest of the federal parks, and was shown running from the Capitol to Washington's Monument in L'Enfant's original plan. Nevertheless, it is only comparatively recently that it has been rearranged along the lines originally proposed.

During the 19th century, the Pennsylvania Railroad Station was on the Mall itself, surrounded by a jumbled mass of shacks (temporary Civil War barracks), assorted gardens, and plots. For a considerable interval, the unfinished pile of the Washington Monument kept them company. Beyond the Monument, there was the largest marsh in the city.

The McMillan Commission of 1902 was the initial moving force behind the present form of the Mall, although the original proposals were more elaborate than those carried out. The reclaiming of the swamp began immediately thereafter, followed in 1922 by the Lincoln Memorial. The Mall is now closer to L'Enfant's vision than ever before. It is lined with many of the city's important art galleries and museums and is a great cultural center as well as a grand axis.

THE WASHINGTON MONUMENT
The Mall
1848–1885 — Robert Mills

"The obelisk has to my eye a singular aptitude in its form and character to call attention to a spot memorable in its history. It says but one work. But it speaks loud. If I understand this voice, it says 'Here!'."
—Horatio Greenough

At 555 feet 5⅛ inches, this is the tallest masonry structure in the world.

Mills' original design, the winner of a competition, called for a circular "Greek" peristyle temple around the base and a more blunt obelisk. Due to geological conditions, it is some 100 yards southwest of the Washington Monument in L'Enfant's plan. The construction period, marked by delays and complications which included the theft of books and records of the Monument society, ran a fitful 37 years.

BUREAU OF ENGRAVING
14th and C Streets, S.W.
1880 — James G. Hill

Originally the Bureau of Printing and Engraving, this Romantic Revival building is still used by the Engraving Division because of its provision for clear north lighting.

3

JEFFERSON MEMORIAL
The Tidal Basin
1943—John Russell Pope, architect
      Rudolph Evans, sculptor
HOURS: 8 A.M. TO 5 P.M. DAILY

There was no site for a Jefferson Memorial on L'Enfant's plan, but then neither had Jefferson been President nor did the site itself exist.

By the time a site had been created, out of river-bottom fill, the heyday of the Classic Revival had already passed and the Memorial seemed somehow, even at its inception, to lack the fire of inspiration which so characterized the man.

4

DEPARTMENT OF AGRICULTURE
14th and Independence Avenue, S.W.
1905—Rankin, Kellogg & Crane

This was the first building begun on the south side of the Mall under the McMillan Commission. Although the foundations were laid in 1905—with great controversy as to the best location—the entire structure was not finally completed until 1930.

5

FREER GALLERY OF ART
12th and Jefferson Drive, S.W.
1923—Charles A. Platt
HOURS: 9 A.M. TO 4:30 P.M.

"The large wall surfaces and restrained handling of Florentine detail serve to denote its function as an art museum."
—Federal Writer's Project *Guide to Washington,* 1937
A simple symmetrical plan with courtyard provides an unobtrusive background for a superlative collection of oriental art and for the work of James A. McN. Whistler.

6

THE SMITHSONIAN BUILDING
Jefferson Drive, between 9th and 12th Streets, S.W.
1849—James Renwick

". . . the business of an American architect is to build something that will stand and be fairly presentable for about thirty years.

—James Renwick

The Smithsonian Institution was founded in 1829 with an unaccountable bequest by an Englishman who had never been to this country. It now encompasses several buildings. This, the oldest, is one of the most important and finest Gothic Revival buildings in America. Built of local Seneca sandstone, it is now administrative head-quarters for the Institution.

7

MUSEUM OF NATURAL HISTORY
Between 9th and 12th Streets, N.W.
(North side of Mall)
1910—Hornblower & Marshall
HOURS: 9 A.M. TO 4:30 P.M. DAILY

This was the first building to be erected along the north side of the Mall in accordance with the McMillan Commission Mall Plan of 1901.

The new neighbor to the south is the Smithsonian's Museum of History and Technology.

8

THE DOWNING MEMORIAL
c. 1864—Calvert Vaux

"Some time after the loss of the Henry Clay a private subscription was raised for the purpose of erecting, in the grounds attached to the Smithsonian Institute at Washington, some fitting memorial of Mr. Downing, who was engaged by the government, at the time of his death, in carrying into execution a comprehensive plan for landscape gardening that included the Smithsonian grounds, and also the whole of the public park proposed to connect the President's house with the Capitol. The design ultimately determined on for this memorial, which is now being erected at Washington, on the site appropriated for the purpose . . . is simply a large, white marble vase, carefully modeled from a chaste but highly enriched antique example, and mounted on an appropriate pedestal."
—Calvert Vaux

Andrew Jackson Downing was the partner of Calvert Vaux at the time of his tragic death in a boat accident.

ARTS AND INDUSTRIES BUILDING
9th and Independence Avenue, S.W.
1880—Cluss and Schulze
HOURS: 9 A.M. TO 4:30 P.M. DAILY

"American architecture is the art of covering one thing with another thing to imitate a third thing, which if genuine would not be desirable."

—Leopold Eidlitz

A fairy-tale castle in polychrome brick, the younger of the Smithsonian Institution's feudal pair cost less than $250,000 total for 2½ acres of floor area or 6 units per cubic foot when built. The great trussed sheds and meandering iron balconies within have a character at once industrial and nostalgic, which seems perfectly appropriate for the Institute's collections.

HIRSHHORN MUSEUM
1974—Skidmore, Owings & Merrill

AIR AND SPACE MUSEUM
1974—Hellmuth, Obata & Kassabaum

Both of these buildings, under construction as this edition of the Guide was prepared, are scheduled for completion in 1974.

NATIONAL GALLERY
6th and Constitution Avenue, N.W.
1941—J. R. Pope

This building is more distinguished for the scale of its halls and rotunda and the quality of materials than for the design itself. Nevertheless, the galleries display the incomparable art collection with great effectiveness.

The National Gallery and the closely related Jefferson Memorial, also by Pope, are the last major eclectic monuments to be erected by the government in the city.

Now under construction is the addition designed by I. M. Pei & Partners, as abstract essay in the acute and oblique.

ANDREW MELLON MEMORIAL FOUNTAIN
6th and Constitution Avenue, N.W.
1952—Eggers and Higgins

D The Federal Triangle

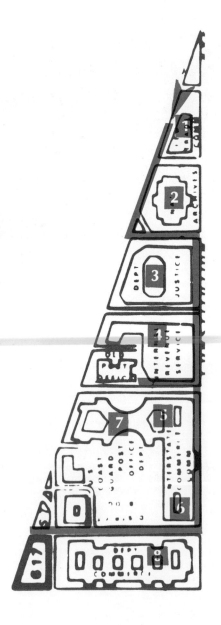

Here is the center of big bureaucratic government in all its official aspects. This monstrous project, with its three-quarter mile runs of governmental eclectic facades, dates from the decade 1928–38.

Before this project, the area was a motley assortment of structures. One of the most notable, shown above, was the now vanished Center Market. The Old District and Post Office Buildings, however, still stand as immovable survivors.

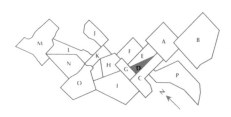

FEDERAL TRADE COMMISSION
6th and Constitution Avenue, N.W.
1937—Bennett, Parsons, Frost

NATIONAL ARCHIVES
8th and Constitution Avenue, N.W.
1935—J. R. Pope
HOURS: 9 A.M. TO 10 P.M.

DEPARTMENT OF JUSTICE
9th and Constitution Avenue, N.W.
1934—Zantzinger, Boris, Medary
HOURS: FBI, 9:15 A.M. TO 4:15 P.M.

INTERNAL REVENUE SERVICE
10th and Constitution Avenue, N.W.
1930–1935—Louis Simon, Architect of Treasury

5

INTERSTATE COMMERCE COMMISSION
12th and Constitution Avenue, N.W.
1935—Arthur Brown

6

DEPARTMENT OF LABOR
14th and Constitution Avenue, N.W.
1935—Arthur Brown

7

POST OFFICE DEPARTMENT
Pennsylvania Avenue between 11th and 12th Streets, N.W.
1934—Delano and Aldrich

8

DEPARTMENT OF COMMERCE
14th Street between E and Constitution Avenue, N.W.
1932—York and Sawyer

Although most buildings of the Federal Triangle are by different architects, they were conceived as a single monumental composition under the guidance of a coordinating committee. Most are six-story buildings, but the fact is generally obscured, if not concealed, by various academic devices. The plans within fulfull the promise of endlessly intersecting corridors. Only the Archives Building, perhaps by virtue of being appropriately a type of mausoleum— free-standing and of great scale—achieves a certain individual success. The other buildings may vary in their handling of elements and details, but they finally melt into one gray strip. It becomes merely incidental, for instance, that the Department of Commerce was the largest office building in the city when completed. But as an immense planned development of cityscape (perhaps the largest in the country), the Federal Triangle bears study.

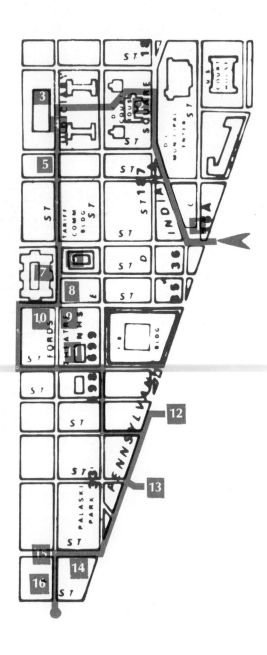

Here is Washington's forgotten architecture, off the tourists' beaten track. These buildings seem somewhat unwelcome reminders of 19th-century America—when the country was small and still struggling. Designed with bravado rather than confidence, they have personalities of their own, most often expressed in their lofty interiors. Those who think of Washington in terms of Beaux-Arts temples in park-like settings may find this individuality disconcerting.

It is inaction, rather than deliberate intention, that has prevented the disappearance of this Washington. The most important buildings in this group are governmental; and the mood of Congress, at least so far as appropriations for Washington architecture are concerned, seems to alternate between delay and reluctance. It takes money even to tear down a building. Fortunately, a new interest is being shown in these buildings, and several are slated for new and glamorous roles.

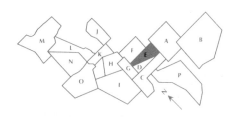

1

TEMPERANCE FOUNTAIN
7th Street and Pennsylvania Avenue, N.W.
1882

> *"Water is best."*
> —Pindar

This fountain, now dry and decorative rather than de-monstrative, was presented to the city by Dr. Henry D. Cogswell, a San Francisco temperance crusader.

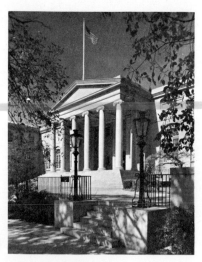

2

D. C. COURTHOUSE
(Old City Hall)
4th and D Streets, N.W.
1820–1850—George Hadfield

A "Grand National Lottery" was the unusual (and un-successful) method of financing. Displaying simple Ionic temple forms typical of the early Greek Revival, this build-ing is also notable for its siting at the end of a short axis perpendicular to Pennsylvania Avenue.

OLD PENSION BUILDING
5th and G Streets, N.W.
1883—General Montgomery Meigs

Once nicknamed "Meigs' Old Red Barn," this is Washington's economy version of the Palazzo Farnese. The frieze, by Bohemian sculptor Casper Buberl, suggesting the Parthenon in cowboy garb, depicts various aspects of life in the Union Army. Inside is the most astonishing room in Washington, for the building is essentially hollow. Built for the dispensing of pensions to Union War Veterans and their relatives, it was used by the Selective Service System until recently when the vast interior space was again opened into one room. Temporarily in use by the District Courts, it is planned to ultimately convert the building to museum use.

OLD PENSION BUILDING

METRO STATION
Judiciary Square
Fourth and E Streets, N.W.
Open 1975 — Harry Weese & Associates Ltd.
INSPECTION TRIPS BY APPOINTMENT

This is the prototype of the underground stations for Washington's new subway system currently under construction.

OPERATIONS CONTROL CENTER BUILDING —
WASHINGTON METROPOLITAN AREA TRANSIT
AUTHORITY
5th Street, N.W., between F and G Streets
1974 — Keyes, Lethbridge and Condon

Here light and void play off against the dark and solid of the Pension Building, opposite.

6

TARIFF COMMISSION
(Old Post Office)
7th and 8th Streets between E and F, N.W.
1839–1869—Robert Mills
HOURS: 9 A.M. TO 4:30 P.M.

This is the least known and least vigorous of the three Classic Revival government departmental buildings with which Mills was involved.

7

NATIONAL PORTRAIT GALLERY
(Old Patent Office)
7th, 9th and G Streets, N.W.
1836–1867—William Elliot, Robert Mills,
    Edward Clark, and others.
1969—Restoration—Faulkner, Stenhouse, Fryer and
    Faulkner. Consultants—Victor Proetz; Bayard
    Underwood

"The public sentiment just now runs almost exclusively and popularly into the Grecian school. We build little besides temples for our churches, our banks, our taverns, our court houses, and our dwellings. A friend of mine has just built a brewery on the model of the Temple of the Winds."
    —Aristabulus Bragg in James Fenimore Cooper's
    Home as Found, 1828.
The porticoes are purported to be exact reproductions of those of the Parthenon in Virginia freestone. In the top-floor model gallery, technology once almost audibly confronted the classic orders. Before being designated for use as the National Portrait Gallery, the Patent Office had been near demolition several times. In L'Enfant's Plan, the site was reserved for a national church and mausoleum.

LE DROIT BUILDING
8th and F Streets, N.W.
1875—A. L. Barber & Co.

This is one of the few remaining Victorian, nonelevator office buildings in this or any other city. The large, north-facing windows—to provide adequate work light in that prefluorescent era—have made this a favorite for artists' studios. In this case the trim is Italianate Revival.

RIGGS BANK
9th and F Streets, N.W.
1891—James G. Hill

Although related closely to Sullivan's Auditorium Building and Richardson's Marshall Field Warehouse, this building lacks the bold changes of scale and willful roughness characteristic of the work of those two architects.

LANSBURGHS FURNITURE STORE
(Old Masonic Hall)
9th and F Streets, N.W.
1867—Cluss and Kammerheuber

A prominent post–Civil War building, designed with shops on the ground floor and Masonic Hall above.

11

FORD'S THEATER
511 10th Street, N.W.
1863—James J. Gifford
1968—Macomber & Peter; Wm. Haussman, restoration

This is the building in which Booth shot Lincoln. Now meticulously restored to near original condition, its stage lights are now lit again. In the basement is a small museum of Lincolniana.

12

OLD POST OFFICE
12th and Pennsylvania Avenue, N.W.
1899—W. Edbrooke

"The body of Romanesque work in this country is now more extensive, and upon the whole, more meritorious than the building of any style which our architects had previously taken as the point of departure for a 'movement,' excepting only the Gothic Revival."

—Montgomery Schuyler, 1891

An independent note in the midst of an otherwise exclusively neo-Classic Federal Triangle, this is one of Washington's few significant Romanesque Revival buildings.

DISTRICT BUILDING
Pennsylvania Avenue at 14th Street, N.W.
1908—Cope and Stewardson

A fine example of the full flower of American Beaux-Arts "classicism," through whose doors one always expects a long-vanished political boss, vest-thumbing and bespatted, to suddenly appear. Only recently has it come to be regarded as an eccentricity rather than a monstrosity.

WILLARD HOTEL
14th and Pennsylvania Avenue, N.W.
1901—Henry Hardenbergh

Although the present building—by the architect of the Plaza Hotel in New York—dates from 1901, there has been a hotel in this location since about 1818. The corner has been host to Presidents and important guests from that time on. The mansarded penthouse—possibly to evade the city's height restriction—is a link to its New York counterparts.

15

JULIUS GARFINCKEL & CO.
14th and F Streets, N.W.
1930—Starrett and van Vleck

The low-key exterior is matched by the open, unhurried, carpet-hushed atmosphere within.

16

OLD EBBITT GRILL
1427 F. Street, N.W.
c. 1890

Although the Old Ebbitt was moved to its present location in 1926, the bar, paneling and decorations, and—most of all—the atmosphere date from the nineteenth century.

F Downtown

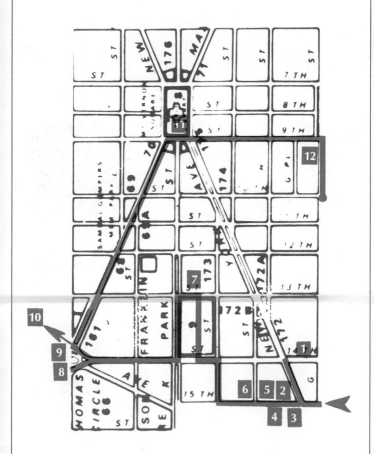

This is not a tour of the downtown shopping area; rather it is a tour of the financial district, appropriately pretentious and clustered around the Treasury—with Thomas Circle and a handful of miscellaneous buildings to round it out. The shopping heart of Washington, which in any other city would be downtown, is nowhere and anywhere. It is a hopeless jumble of pop culture. No official tour is included.

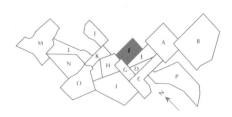

COLORADO BUILDING
14th and G Streets, N.W.
1922—Ralph S. Townsend
　　The decoration here is a veritable architectural garden —with eagles and lions standing guard.

NATIONAL SAVINGS AND TRUST COMPANY
15th and New York Avenue, N.W.
1880—James Windrim

　　Complex fenestration and an unusual and, in places, peculiar mixture of ornamental devices mark this structure. Against its Banker's Classic neighbors it provides one of the strong architectural juxtapositions so common in Washington.

AMERICAN SECURITY AND TRUST CO.
15th and Pennsylvania Avenue, N.W.
1899—York and Sawyer

RIGGS NATIONAL BANK
1503 Pennsylvania Avenue, N.W.
1898—York and Sawyer

"'How did the hard common-sense man come to think of a Roman Temple? How did common sense manage to get in its deadly work?'
"'Why, easy enough. His architect made a picture of what he thought was a Roman temple, and showed it to the banker, telling him on the side that Roman temples were rather the go now for banks, and the banker bit. That's plain enough, isn't it?'"
—Louis Sullivan, *Kindergarten Chats,* 1918

These buildings combine their massive columns with those of the Treasury to give Washington's financial district a distinct, if rather stolid, ambiance.

UNION TRUST BUILDING
S.W. corner of 15th and H Streets, N.W.
1906—Wood, Donn and Deming

5

FOLGER BUILDING AND PLAYHOUSE THEATER
715–725 15th Street, N.W.
1906—Folger Building—J. H. de Sibour
         Playhouse Theater—Paul Pelz

"He marks—not what you won or lost—but how you played the game."

—Grantland Rice

This swashbuckling Beaux-Arts tour-de-force has a bravado which renders criticism useless.

6

SOUTHERN BUILDING
1425 H Street, N.W.
1912—D. H. Burnham & Associates

    The careful alignment of cornices and belt-courses, as well as the ground-level pilasters and columns of neighboring buildings, gives a continuity to this block in spite of individual differences. The winged plan—designed to give light and air—is typical of large Washington office and apartment buildings of the time.

FRANKLIN SCHOOL
13th and K Streets, N.W.
1868—Adolph Cluss

A model of advanced school design in its day, the Franklin School received honors both abroad and at home. Now abandoned by the offices of the Superintendent of Schools, a new adaptive use for the building is desperately needed.

NATIONAL CITY CHRISTIAN CHURCH
14th and Massachusetts Avenue, N.W. (Thomas Circle)
1930—John Russell Pope
1952—Addition by Leon Chatelain, Jr.

American colonial churches and the work of Inigo Jones are recalled here at a scale which is larger than life-size. Since the church is on a small mound as well, it completely dominates the circle.

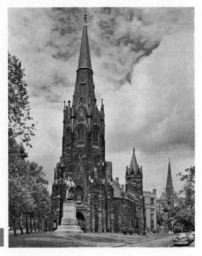

9

LUTHER PLACE MEMORIAL CHURCH
1226 Vermont Avenue, N.W. (Thomas Circle)
1870—Judson York
1952—Addition by L. M. Leisenring

Neo-Gothic in red sandstone, this church was built as a memorial of thanksgiving for the ending of the Civil War. With the National City Christian Church across the street, we have one period piece flanking another.

10

LOGAN CIRCLE
1875–1900

The Logan Circle area is a good example of the fact that neglect is often the handmaiden of preservation.

This is an eight block area of virtually unchanged large, late-nineteenth-century Victorian and Richardsonian houses focusing on the Circle itself.

Nearly all were constructed during the twenty-five-year period between 1875 and 1900 as the homes of the prominent and wealthy. By the mid-eighteen-nineties taste had shifted and the Dupont Circle area had become the fashionable district, but, almost incredibly, only three of the original houses on the Circle have been demolished in the twentieth century.

CENTRAL LIBRARY
8th and K Streets, N.W.
1902—Ackerman and Ross

The main entrance on New York Avenue is stolid Beaux-Arts, but the functional demands of the library within break through the facade as one moves around the building. Unexpectedly, the center bay of the rear facade is a bold arrangement of slots for lighting the book stacks.

MARTIN LUTHER KING MEMORIAL LIBRARY
(New D.C. Central Library)
901 G Street, N.W.
1972—The Office of Mies van der Rohe
HOURS: 9 A.M. TO MIDNIGHT, MONDAY THRU FRIDAY
9 A.M. TO 5:30 P.M., SATURDAY
1 P.M. TO 5 P.M., SUNDAY

"Black is beautiful."

—Anonymous

This traditional Miesian package is his only work in the area. His being commissioned by the city rather than a private client says a great deal about the architectural aspirations of corporate Washington.

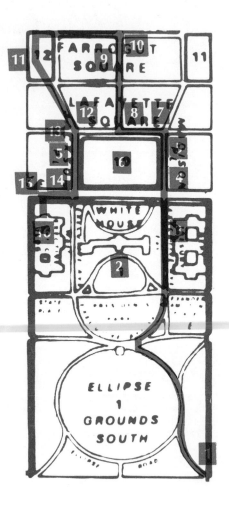

St. John's Church, in the city of Washington, with the President's house as it appeared in 1816, when the Church was built.

Henry Adams once remarked, *"Beyond the square the country began."*

Adams resided on the square longer than anyone else, and his death in 1918 marked the end of its great period as the center of the country's social, intellectual, scientific, and political life.

When L'Enfant selected his site for the President's house, the area was an orchard. With the White House as a focal point, it soon developed as the location for court residences. Decatur House and the Cutts-Madison House were the beginning; H. H. Richardson's houses for Henry Adams and John Hay—now the site of the Hay-Adams Hotel—were the last of these residences.

By the turn of the century, the residential character of the Square was changing, and Massachusetts Avenue had become the fashionable residential area of the moment.

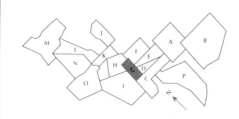

CAPITOL GATEHOUSE
N.W. cor. 15th and Constitution Avenue, N.W.
c. 1818—Charles Bulfinch

Bulfinch in an unusual ornate vein. These gatehouses were moved here from their original location on Capitol Hill.

THE WHITE HOUSE
1600 Pennsylvania Avenue, N.W.
Begun 1792—James Hoban, Benjamin H. Latrobe and others
HOURS: 10 A.M. TO 12, EXCEPT SUNDAY, MONDAY AND HOLIDAYS

"The Palace . . . should stand in the Heart of a City, it should be easy of access, beautifully adorned, and rather delicate and polite . . ."
—Leone Battista Alberti, *Ten Books on Architecture,*
Leoni, 1755

An early 19th century print showing the White House in 1807 as built by James Hoban.

1792—James Hoban, an Irish architect practicing in Charleston, South Carolina, was declared winner of the competition for the design of the President's House and awarded a gold medal worth $500. He triumphed over, among others, Thomas Jefferson, who had made an anonymous submission. Hoban's design appears to have been influenced by Leinster House, Dublin, and James Gibb's *Book of Architecture.*

Construction was begun immediately, but the building was still unfinished when the government moved from Philadelphia in November 1800 and the Adamses took possession. Abigail Adams wrote her daughter:

"The house is made habitable but there is not a single apartment finished . . . We have not the least fence, yard, or other convenience, without, and the great unfinished audience-room [the East Room] I make a drying room of, to hang up the clothes in."

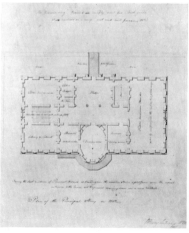

Plan of the "principal story" drawn for Thomas Jefferson by B. H. Latrobe showing the White House as originally built.

1807—Jefferson, who described the house as "big enough for two emperors, one Pope and the grand Lama," collaborated with Latrobe to add a low terrace-pavilion on either side of the main building.

Drawing by W. Strickland showing the burned out White House soon after the "conflagration of the 24th of August 1814."

1814—Set afire by the British in August, the House was saved from total destruction by a violent thunderstorm which quenched the flames.

1815—While President Madison lived in the Octagon House, Hoban reproduced the original building. It is possible that the building—of Virginia sandstone, not marble—was first painted white at this time to cover charring from the fire. However, the term "White House" may date from before 1812.

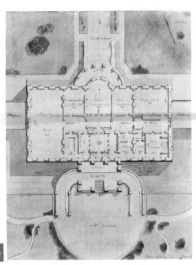

B. H. Latrobe's revised White House design made for Thomas Jefferson in 1807. Hoban's later re-building closely followed Latrobe's scheme.

1824—The semicircular South Portico was added by Hoban. This appears to combine his original design with that submitted by Latrobe for Jefferson's consideration in 1807.

2f

The south elevation of Latrobe's 1807 proposal drawn in 1817. St. John's Church is in the background at right.

1829—Following Latrobe's drawings, Hoban completed the North Portico.

1848—Gas lighting was installed.

1849—Andrew Jackson Downing planned the White House grounds. Much of his work still remains.

1853—City water was supplied.

c. 1878—Bathrooms were added.

c. 1890—Electric service was introduced.

c. 1900—Several schemes for greatly expanding and altering the White House were proposed and dismissed.

1902—McKim, Mead and White extensively remodeled the original building, removed the conservatories, and added the East Gallery and Executive Office wing. The latter has been successively enlarged since, and the old State, War and Navy building was finally taken over to add needed space.

1949–52—During the Truman administration, the White House was found to be structurally unsound. Although the exterior walls were left standing, the entire inner structure was removed and replaced with steel framing. The original paneling, trim and decorations were reinstalled. Lorenzo Winslow served as White House architect.

3

TREASURY BUILDING
1500 Pennsylvania Avenue, N.W.
1836–1869—Robert Mills, Thomas Ustick Walter

> *". . . with wheel-tracks meandering from the colonnade of the Treasury hard by, to the white marble [sic] columns and fronts of the Post Office and Patent Office which faced each other in the distance, like white Greek temples in the abandoned gravel-pits of a deserted Syrian City."*
> —Henry Adams, c. 1850

Robert Mills, who had been a draughtsman for both Latrobe and Jefferson, was at least partially responsible for all three buildings mentioned by Adams.

Site planning for the Treasury was by Andrew Jackson who said "Build it here!" thus obliterating L'Enfant's vista from the Capitol to the White House. It is the oldest of the government's departmental buildings.

4

TREASURY ANNEX
S.E. corner of Lafayette Square, N.W.
1919—Cass Gilbert

5a

LAFAYETTE SQUARE RECONSTRUCTION
East—UNITED STATES COURT OF CLAIMS
    717 Madison Place, N.W.
    1968—John Carl Warnecke and Associates
HOURS: 9 A.M. TO 5 P.M., MONDAY THRU FRIDAY

Another scheme razing the row houses along Lafayette Square had already been designed when President Kennedy asked architect Warnecke to study the problem. While the tall buildings behind are certainly more dominant than all would have wished, the scale and fabric of Lafayette Square were not only saved but enchanced. Furthermore, it is a scheme—high elements in the center of a block behind a wall of row houses—with obvious application elsewhere.

5b

LAFAYETTE SQUARE RECONSTRUCTION
West—NEW EXECUTIVE OFFICE BUILDING
    17th and Pennsylvania Avenue, N.W.
    1968—John Carl Warnecke and Associates
HOURS: 9 A.M. TO 5 P.M., MONDAY THRU FRIDAY

6

JACKSON STATUE
Lafayette Square
1855—Clark Mills

"*I remember a short spring-time of years ago when Lafayette Square, itself, contiguous to the Executive Mansion, could create a rich sense of the past by the use of scarce other witchcraft than its command of that pleasant perspective and its possession of the most prodigious of all Presidential effigies, Andrew Jackson, as archaic as a Ninevite king, prancing and rocking through the ages.*"
—Henry James, *The American Scene*

Cannon captured by Jackson in the War of 1812 supplied the bronze. Mills actually trained a horse to remain in a rearing position for study; Jackson's head is based on contemporary portraits.

7

ST. JOHN'S PARISH BUILDING
(Old British Embassy)
1525 H Street, N.W.
1822–1834—St. Clair Clarke, Owner

8

ST. JOHN'S CHURCH
16th and H Streets, N.W.
1816—Benjamin H. Latrobe
1883—James Renwick

By tradition, pew 54 has been set aside for the President and his family. Latrobe's Church was a Greek cross in plan. The extended nave, portico, and steeple are subsequent additions of 1820 by other architects. Latrobe himself was the first organist and donated his architectural services.

9

THIRD CHURCH OF CHRIST, SCIENTIST
& THE CHRISTIAN SCIENCE MONITOR BUILDING
16th and Eye Streets, N.W.
1972—I. M. Pei and Partners
SERVICES WITH TOURS AFTER: 12 NOON AND 8 P.M., WEDS.
11 A.M. AND 5 P.M., SUNDAY

Primary sculpture at architectural scale, this is one of a number of complexes by this architect for this client.

While the plaza has been criticized as unnecessary here on 16th Street, the tension of tower, wall and octagon make this, perhaps, the most satisfying new complex in the city.

The simplicity of form and opening are carried off by exposed-concete work which gives lie to the theory that architectural craftsmanship is a dead art.

10

SHERATON-CARLTON HOTEL
16th and K Streets, N.W.
1926—Mihran Mesrobian

This elegant small hotel is particularly noted for its public spaces within.

11

BARR BUILDING
910 17th Street, N.W.
1930—Stanley Simmons

The clear expression of the window module and structural bay and the elaboration of the base give an interest and organization to which the neo-Gothic ornament is incidental. The newer, neighboring office buildings are a convenient contrast to the gray stone network.

CHAMBER OF COMMERCE BUILDING
1615 H Street, N.W.
1925—Cass Gilbert

An interesting comment on the vagaries of taste: The Chamber of Commerce and Treasury Annex buildings are the only completed portions of a plan to unify the architecture of Lafayette Square in the manner of the older Treasury Department. It had also been proposed that the Executive Office Building (Old State, War and Navy) be remodeled to conform.

DECATUR HOUSE
Northwest corner of Lafayette Square, N.W.
1818—Benjamin H. Latrobe
HOURS: 12 TO 5 P.M. DAILY

Latrobe's house for Commodore Stephen Decatur, suppressor of the Barbary pirates, is particularly noted for the proportion of its interiors. This, the first private house to be built on Lafayette Square, the White House, and St. John's Church form a trio of Latrobe's work.

BLAIR-LEE HOUSES
1650 Pennsylvania Avenue, N.W.
1824
1931—Restored, Waldron Faulkner

Blair-Lee Houses are now government property and are used for entertaining distinguished visitors from other countries.

RENWICK GALLERY
(Old Corcoran Gallery and Court of Claims)
17th Street and Pennsylvania Avenue, N.W.
1859—James Renwick
1972—J. C. Warnecke and Associates, exterior restoration
**   H. N. Jacobsen, interior restoration and remodeling**

It took William Wilson Corcoran some 14 years to be able to occupy his own building. Just as it was completed, the Civil War broke out and the government borrowed it. When he finally took possession, the building had become too small for his collection, and he had to have a new, larger gallery built down 17th Street.

The large open galleries, however, were easily converted into court rooms and judges' chambers, and the building became the Court of Claims.

With its facade painstakingly restored and the interiors once again predominantly Victorian, the building has now been returned to its original function as a gallery.

16a

EXECUTIVE OFFICE BUILDING
(Old State, War and Navy)
Pennsylvania Avenue and 17th Street, N.W.
1871–1888—A. B. Mullett

16b

EXECUTIVE OFFICE BUILDING

At the time that it was built, this was the world's largest office building. Henry Adams called it Mr. Mullett's "architectural infant asylum." Behind the 900 doric columns are some surprises: at each corner a heroic cantilevered stairway spirals down and, buried within the vastness of the interior, is a pair of libraries—perforated fantasies of cast iron. There have been a number of schemes in the past for remodeling this building to match the Treasury Building.

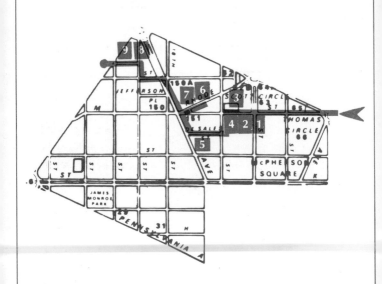

VIEW OF THE CITY OF WASHINGTON

Connecticut Avenue, one of Washington's grand thoroughfares, cuts through from Lafayette Square to Chevy Chase, Maryland, and beyond. Once a fashionable residential area, the relatively few remaining houses have been converted to business use. Its shops have traditionally been among the city's most elegant but the prolonged construction of the subway along this route is testing the endurance of many.

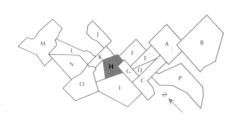

METROPOLITAN A.M.E. CHURCH
1518 M Street, N.W.
1885—Samuel T. Morsell
HOURS: 9:30 A.M. TO 3:30 P.M., MONDAY THRU FRIDAY

Architecturally significant as an example of brick Gothic Revival, the church is also a landmark of the black civil rights movement.

HUBBARD MEMORIAL LIBRARY
1146 16th Street, N. W.
1902—Hornblower and Marshall

SUMNER SCHOOL
17th and M Streets, N.W.
1871–1872—Adolph Cluss

Mutilated by the decapitation of its clock tower, Sumner is still an important survivor of the city's nineteenth-century school architecture.

4

NATIONAL GEOGRAPHIC SOCIETY
17th and M Streets, N.W.
1964—Edward Durell Stone
HOURS: 9 A.M. TO 7 P.M. WEEKDAYS
9 A.M. TO 5 P.M. SATURDAYS
12 TO 5 SUNDAYS

The lid roof, recessed top floors, and close fence of vertical shafts would appear to make this the descendant of Frank Lloyd Wright's project for the Press Building in San Francisco.

5

MAYFLOWER HOTEL
1127 Connecticut Avenue, N.W.
1924—Warren & Wetmore, Robert S. Beresford

For over a half a century this hotel has been host to itinerant power. Built in American hotel style of the twenties with French appliqué, it offers a grand parade of an interior street through its lobby.

6

ST. MATTHEW'S CATHEDRAL
1725 Rhode Island Avenue, N.W.
1899—Heins and LaFarge

The rather confectionery interiors contrast strongly with the clear geometry and plain brick surfaces of the exterior.

7

LONGFELLOW BUILDING
1741 Rhode Island Avenue, N.W.
1940—William Lescaze

"'It's very rude of him,' she said,
'To come and spoil the fun!'"
— Lewis Carroll, *Through the Looking Glass*

This is Washington's first modern office building and one of the first anywhere to separate the service core from the office space and express it as a vertical shaft.

8

SUNDERLAND BUILDING
1320 19th Street, N.W.
1969—Keyes, Lethbridge & Condon

A relatively small, foursquare, professional office building of buff-colored, poured-in-place concrete. Recessed,
narrow windows surround the building on all sides, flanked
by columns and duct enclosures angled to enlarge the view
in one direction while shielding the glass from the hottest
sun.

9

COLUMBIA HISTORICAL SOCIETY
(Heurich House)
1307 New Hampshire Avenue, N.W. (at 20th Street)
1880—J. G. Myers

Knotty and somewhat apprehensive, this house also
stakes out a corner in the domestic architecture of the city
as an unmatched example of Victorian grandeur. Intact and
original, the shadowy interiors as well are a museum of
their time. It is now the home of the Columbia Historical
Society.

17th Street to Memorial Bridge

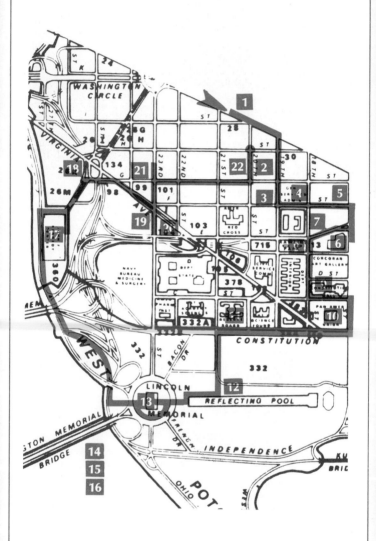

This walk beneath the great elms along 17th Street is one of the most pleasant in the city. With the splendors of the Renaissance style facing the shaded expanse of the Ellipse as it sweeps to meet the Mall, the traditions of Washington as a city of white monumental buildings in a park-like setting are never more apparent.

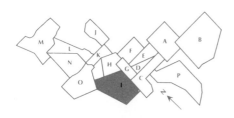

ARTS CLUB
2017 1 Street, N.W.
1802–1806—Timothy Caldwell, owner-builder

Caldwell's avowed intention was to build "the handsomest house in the capital city." However, the construction cost was so great that he was forced to sell it shortly after completion. Biding his time, he then bought it back in 1813. It has been the home of the Arts Club since 1916.

INTERNATIONAL MONETARY FUND BUILDING
19th and G Streets, N.W.
1973—Vincent G. Kling & Partners in Association with
Clas, Riggs, Owens & Ramos
HOURS: INTERIOR LOBBY—9 A.M. TO 5 P.M. DAILY

, A massive and magnificent interior courtyard provides windows for a maximum number of offices and a 110-by-120-foot, two-level, air-conditioned plaza for receptions and exhibitions.

3

LENTHALL HOUSES
612 and 614 19th Street, N.W.
C. 1800

John Lenthall, Benjamin Latrobe's principal assistant in his work on the U.S. Capitol, was the first owner of these houses. Lenthall was killed in September of 1808 when one of the arches in the Supreme Court Chamber of the Capitol collapsed and crushed him.

4

JOHN MARSHALL HOUSE
1801 F Street, N.W.
1825—Tench Ringgold, owner-builder

This house has been occupied by John Marshall, Presidents Madison and Van Buren, and Major General McClellan.

5

WINDER BUILDING
604 17th Street, N.W.
1847–1848

When built, this building pioneered the use of central heating and steel beams and was a veritable high-rise in its time. The facade has been altered, but the importance of the building is historical rather than architectural, it being the first of a hardy Washington breed—the cheap speculative office building designed to be leased to the Federal Government.

6

CORCORAN GALLERY OF ART
17th and New York Avenue, N.W.
1897—Ernest Flagg
1927—Charles Platt
HOURS: 10 A.M. TO 4:30 P.M. WEEKDAYS
2 P.M. TO 5 P.M. SATURDAYS AND SUNDAYS

". . . for whatever has once genuinely pleased is likely to be again found pleasing; art and the enjoyment of art continue in the condemned paths undismayed; and criticism is left to discover a sanction for them, if it can, in some new theory, as simple, as logical, and as insufficient as the first."

—Geoffrey Scott, *The Architecture of Humanism,* 1914

This is the second Corcoran Gallery, built when the original, now the Court of Claims, was outgrown. But this building also proved too small and was enlarged in 1927 to receive the Clark Collection. The clear articulation of each block, the uncompromising elevations (including those of the addition), and the magnificent interior atrium galleries show the Beaux-Arts tradition at its best.

7

OCTAGON HOUSE
1741 New York Avenue, N.W.
1800—Dr. William Thornton
Open to the public
HOURS: 10 A.M. TO 5 P.M. DAILY, EXCEPT MONDAYS

HEADQUARTERS BUILDING, THE AMERICAN
INSTITUTE OF ARCHITECTS
1735 Pennsylvania Avenue, N.W.
1973—The Architects Collaborative

Wrapped around the site of the older residence, the new Headquarters Building acts as a shield from other development to the north and east. It replaced a lower office structure built in 1940, the remodeled stable and the Lemon Building, a nineteenth-century office building on the adjoining site.

Still proudly standing, the Octagon House is, itself, an object lesson in the art of nonrectangular planning, here · provoked by one of L'Enfant's oblique intersections.

While the White House was being rebuilt after the fire of 1814, the Octagon House was occupied by President Madison.

8

RAWLINS PARK
E Street between 18th and 19th Streets, N.W.

Particularly when the magnolias are in bloom, this urban park must be the standard to which all should aspire. Its beauty and gentility are easily matched by its popularity.

9

CONSTITUTION HALL
1778 D Street, N.W.
c. 1930—John Russell Pope

Excellent circulation is afforded here by the triple front-age which permits entrances on three sides—the carriage ramp on the north side being the most notable. Within, these entrances are connected by a grand promenade.

10

PAN-AMERICAN UNION
(Organization of American States)
17th and Constitution Avenue, N.W.
1910—Albert Kelsey and Paul Cret
HOURS: 8:30 A.M. TO
4:30 P.M. WEEKDAYS AND SATURDAYS

Combined here are qualities unusual in a single building: imposing formality and inviting elegance. It is also a blending of the architectural styles of North and South America. Within is a patio resplendent with tropical plants and birds.

At the corner of C and 18th Streets stands the stable of the Van Ness Mansion by Benjamin Latrobe, a relic of the famous house which formerly occupied the site.

11

FEDERAL RESERVE BUILDING
Constitution Avenue and 20th Street, N.W.
1937—Paul Cret

Typical of Cret's work of the period in its elegant, stripped classicism, neither modern nor revival, this building along with his Folger Library (A-12) and the nearby Pan American Union (I-10) represent the best of the academic tradition of the thirties.

12

REFLECTING POOL
The Mall
c. 1920—Henry Bacon, Charles McKim, and others.

The McMillan Plan of 1901 called for a cruciform pool between the Washington and Lincoln Memorials, but the so-called "temporary" Navy and Munitions Buildings along Constitution Avenue, which were put up during the First World War, encroached upon the area set aside for the north arm of the pool. The pool was accordingly redesigned as now seen: a long, rectangular basin with a small, transverse pool at its eastern end.

13

LINCOLN MEMORIAL
West Potomac Park (West end of Mall)
1922—Henry Bacon
1922—Statue of Lincoln by Daniel Chester French, sculptor

"Where classic power once stood, its shadow lingered."
—Geoffrey Scott, *The Architecture of Humanism,* 1914
Standing as it does on swamp land reclaimed under the McMillan Park Commission, the Lincoln Memorial is an element in Washington's monumental composition unenvisioned by L'Enfant. On the main axis of the Mall, it counterbalances the Capitol about the Washington Monument. The building itself differs from the Greek Temple form in several respects: the replacement of the classic pedimented roof with a recessed attic, and the placement of the entrance at the side are two of the more significant. The latter device enabled the building to be placed at right angles to the Mall and more effectively terminate the axis. White and solemn, the Lincoln Memorial attains a nobility which far transcends its eclectic heritage.

14

ARLINGTON MEMORIAL BRIDGE
1926–1932—McKim, Mead and White

A bridge was proposed at this point as early as 1851, and the present bridge closely follows one suggested by the McMillan Commission in 1901. However, not until (reportedly) a traffic jam en route to the Tomb of the Unknown Soldier on Armistice Day, 1921 made the need self-evident, was the bridge begun. As completed, the bridge project completely transformed the adjacent areas on both sides of the river into a coherent visual and, no less important, automotive experience. It is now one of Washington's major traffic interchanges.

15

ARLINGTON HOUSE
(Custis-Lee Mansion)
Arlington National Cemetery
Arlington, Virginia
1812—George W. P. Custis
1820—George Hadfield
1925—L. M. Leisenring

"It is one of earliest and most notable of the houses of the Greek Revival."

—Fiske Kimball

Early and severe Doric Greek Revival, the portico is based on the temple of Poseidon at Paestum. Directly in front is the tomb of Pierre L'Enfant, and beyond, a magnificent view of the city.

16a

ARLINGTON NATIONAL CEMETERY
Arlington, Virginia
Memorial Amphitheatre
1920—Carrère & Hastings
Tomb of the Unknown Soldier
1931—Lorimer Rich
Thomas Hudson Jones, sculptor

16b

MEMORIAL GATE
1926–1932—McKim, Meade & White

16c

JOHN F. KENNEDY GRAVE
1966—John Carl Warnecke & Associates
Visitors welcome

JOHN F. KENNEDY CENTER FOR THE PERFORMING ARTS
2700 F Street, N.W.
1969—Edward Durell Stone

Despite criticism of its location, scale and form, the Center has undeniably succeeded in bringing a much richer cultural fare to the Nation's Capital. Among those features of the Center which have merited special praise have been the acoustics of the performing halls and the willow-shaded terrace along the river facade, which make an intermission interlude (weather permitting) most pleasant.

THE WATERGATE
2500, 2600, 2700 Virginia Avenue, N.W.
600, 700 New Hampshire Avenue, N.W.
1964–1972—Luigi Moretti, architect
Corning, Moore, Elmore and Fisher, associate architects

The convolutions of Moretti's plan have a certain inner (and outer) logic—the outer logic being a restless form that fills the oddly shaped site yet reduces the aggregate bulk of the buildings; the inner logic being a succession of partially enclosed courts and a great variety of aspects and views. Some of the detailing borders upon the eccentric, but is generally consistent with the baroque quality of the whole complex.

19

COLUMBIA PLAZA
2400 Virginia Avenue, N.W.
1962—Keyes, Lethbridge and Condon, architects
DeMars and Reay, associate architects

An ambitious and complex urban renewal project that was plagued from its inception by recurring squabbles among a succession of owners. The site, bounded and reshaped by the construction of the E Street Expressway, occupies a commanding view of the city and the river, but the original design and site plan were only partially realized, a central hotel and interconnecting plazas having been replaced by a bulkier, less articulated office building.

20

PAN AMERICAN HEALTH ORGANIZATION
525 23rd Street, N.W.
1964—Roman Fresnedo-Siri, design architect
Justement, Elam, Callmer and Kidd, architects

Winner of an inter-American architectural competition, the building group was designed by a Uruguayan architect, assisted by an established Washington firm in its execution. The curved tower and circular conference center complement one another in an unorthodox solution to the special problems of a narrow triangular site.

ST. MARY'S EPISCOPAL CHURCH
730 23rd Street, N.W.
1887—Renwick, Aspinwall & Russell

Originally housed in a relocated Civil War barracks on this same site, the history of St. Mary's is an interesting episode in black ecclesiastical history. The interior of the church is notable for its painted-glass windows, made in France, representing St. Simon, the Cyrenian, St. Tryphoena; and St. Cyprian, the African bishop and martyr.

GEORGE WASHINGTON UNIVERSITY LAW LIBRARY
718 20th Street, N.W.
1970—Mills, Petticord and Mills

A relatively small building in its external appearance—within, it is almost as deep as it is high. The dark brick facade is distinctive for its monochromatic color range and sculptural modeling.

J Meridian Hill

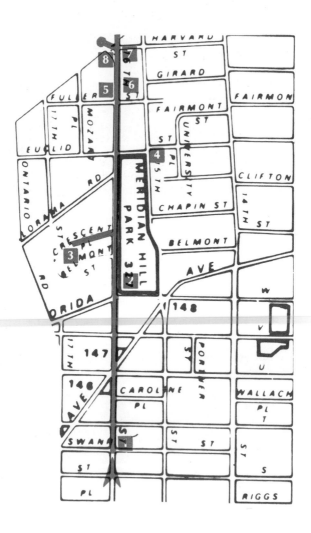

CAMP MERIDIAN HILL
7ᵗʰ REGᵗ N.JERSEY VOLˢ

In everything but name, 16th Street is a grand avenue. Mrs. John B. Henderson, a Washington hostess of 1880–1920, spread her influence as a developer, lobbyist and donor in order to make this street truly the "Avenue of the Presidents." With architect George Oakley Totten, she developed five blocks on the grand scale, in the hope of wooing projects away from Dupont Circle and Massachusetts Avenue to the heights of 16th Street. To the great advantage of the city, Mrs. Henderson's rivalry with the other avenues ended in a draw. Without her magnificent efforts, one might well assume that the present elegance of 16th Street would not exist and Massachusetts Avenue would be overcrowded.

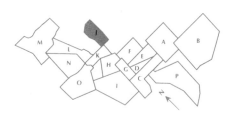

TEMPLE OF THE SCOTTISH RITE
16th and S Streets, N.W.
1910—John Russell Pope

"Most of the stone a nation hammers goes toward its tomb only. It buries itself alive."
—Henry David Thoreau, *Walden*, 1854
Here Pope chose the Tomb of Mausolus at Halicarnassus as his precedent.

MERIDAN HILL PARK
16th Street between Euclid and Florida Avenues, N.W.
1920—Horace Peaslee, architect
        George Burnap, landscape architect

Two areas, contrasting in design and character, comprise the park. The lover level, the Italian section, has for its axis a cascade of 13 graduated pools and falls. The upper level, the French section, dead flat for some 900 feet despite the hill, centers on a broad grass mall. Luxuriant planting shields and detaches the park from the adjoining neighborhood. Particularly notable is the material—exposed aggregate concrete—used throughout for the massive retaining walls, walks, and basins alike.

3

WASHINGTON INTERNATIONAL CENTER
(Meridian House)
1630 Crescent Place, N.W.
1915—John Russell Pope

There is a richness of both space and decor in this house which is sometimes lacking in Pope's later work. This is a house capable of summoning visions of a vanished Society. Complementing the house, the surrealistic pruned trees and gravelled garden are cultivated beyond nature.

4

ECUADORIAN EMBASSY
2535 15th Street, N.W.
1922—George Oakley Totten, Jr.

One of the dozen or so residences designed by Totten and built by Mrs. John B. Henderson, widow of a prominent senator, in a successful effort to develop the area as a center for legations. This particular building has also served other countries. This group includes 2401 and 2437 15th St., 2600 16th St. (see following) and the Spanish Embassy on the corner of 16th and Fuller Streets, all in sympathetic architectural styles.

5

INTER-AMERICAN DEFENSE BOARD
(Pink Palace)
2600 16th Street, N.W.
1906—George Oakley Totten, Jr.

This Venetian-Gothic mansion was the first of the buildings completed by the Henderson-Totten team.

6

LUTHERAN CHURCH CENTER
(Warder-Totten House)
2633 16th Street, N.W.
1885—H. H. Richardson
1902—George Oakley Totten, Jr. (reconstruction)

The design of this house is known to have been in the hands of Richardson's employees, Shepley and Coolidge. The pale, smooth sandstone, rather than Richardson's more characteristic rough granite or sandstone, and the use of a number of 16th century French devices are more than likely due to their influence.

The house was originally built on K Street, between 15th and 16th Streets, N.W. Totten, himself a pupil of Richardson's, bought the remains from the wrecker in 1902 and reconstructed the house on its present site for his own use.

7

ALL SOULS UNITARIAN CHURCH
16th and Harvard Square, N.W.
1924—Coolidge and Shattuck

St. Martins-in-the-Fields, London, by James Gibbs, was the architectural precedent here.

8

CHURCH OF LATTER DAY SAINTS
16th and Harvard Square, N.W.
1933—Young and Hansen

The design of this Mormon Church reflects the Tabernacle in Salt Lake City, Utah. The delicate, linear detailing of the stratified stone skin and consistent verticality—capped by the Angel Moroni—make this one of the most elegant small churches in the city. Its scale is particularly apparent in contrast with the other churches across the street. The interiors, unfortunately, are less distinguished.

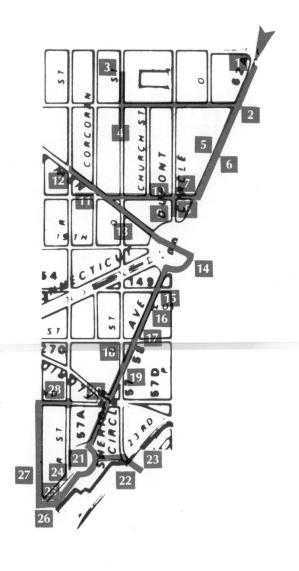

Around the turn of the century, this section of the city
became *the* place to live. It was here, during the years 1900
to 1903, that eight of the city's most magnificent houses
were under construction simultaneously. The American
villa-in-town and the Renaissance Palace—French, English
or Italian—are present and in force. The avenues and
streets radiating from this park within the circle form a
distinct area whose elegant past is ever present through its
architecture. The park was designed by Henry Bacon in
1921, and the fountain memorial to Admiral Du Pont, by
Daniel Chester French.

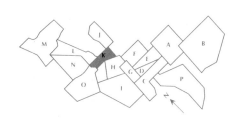

1

FOREST INDUSTRIES BUILDING
1619 Massachusetts Avenue, N.W.
1961—Keyes, Lethbridge and Condon

The ordered restraint of the light-colored concrete frame and the deep-set, contrasting wood windows give a dignity and three-dimensional quality. The recessed entrance court provides a solution to the problem of obtaining a vertical building within the city's rigid height regulations.

2

PERUVIAN CHANCERY
(Wilkins' house)
1700 Massachusetts Avenue
1909—Jules Henri de Sibour

Like Thorton's Octagon House a hundred years earlier, the Wilkins' house copes successfully with the tapering corner lot, an inheritance from L'Enfant's radial avenues. Jules de Sibour was among the first of the Paris-trained architects who brought the Beaux-Arts style to Massachusetts Avenue. He maintained a successful practice in Washington for more than twenty years, producing a substantial number of buildings that are notable for their quality of design.

3

CAIRO HOTEL
1615 Q Street, N.W.
1894—Thomas Franklin Schneider

Neo-Moorish decorative detail was applied to the front facade of the Cairo, one of the earliest high-rise, steel-frame, residential buildings in the United States. The building's height of 160 feet, in an otherwise low-profiled neighborhood, shocked city residents and Congress into establishing height limitations for the District of Columbia. One must admire Schneider's nerve; he built and owned the building—the first, and last, of its kind.

4

SCHNEIDER ROW HOUSES
1700 block of Q Street, N.W.
1889—Thomas Franklin Schneider

"The young Napoleon of F Street." That is the term applied to a certain young architect in this city by his friends. *"Why it's just a few years ago that I was going to school with him playing 'Old Man' and buying a cent's worth of taffy, which we divided at recess,"* said an acquaintance. And it was just last Saturday that the young Napoleon paid $175,000 for a row of lots on Q Street, occupying the whole front of the square between Seventeenth and Eighteenth Streets.—He is a young looking man, with a slight moustache, and a modest retiring air, but he certainly is what the Westerners call a "hustler."
—Washington *Evening News,* November 5, 1889

5

GEORGETOWN UNIVERSITY RESEARCH CENTER
1717 Massachusetts Avenue, N.W.
1964—Cooper and Auerbach

The elevation treatment is a serious attempt to be compatible with the existing buildings on the street, both old and new, through scale and visual interest. The entrance and parking access, in particular, are skillfully handled.

6

CANADIAN CHANCERY
(Moore residence)
1746 Massachusetts Avenue, N.W.
1906—Jules Henri de Sibour

The original owner, Clarence Moore, was a noted horseman—Master of the Hounds of the Chevy Chase Club. He enjoyed the house, one of the finest ever built in the city, for only a few years after its completion, having the misfortune to book passage on the *Titanic* for his return from England in 1912. The former residence, distinguished by its remarkable interior panelling and hardware, has been preserved and well maintained by the Canadian government since 1927.

7

McCORMICK APARTMENTS
1785 Massachusetts Avenue, N.W.
1917—Jules Henri de Sibour

Now converted to office use, these apartments (one per floor) were once the largest and most desirable in the city, occupied by a procession of nabobs, including Andrew Mellon and Lord Duveen.

8

SULGRAVE CLUB
(Wadsworth house)
1801 Massachusetts Avenue, N.W.
c. 1900—Architect unknown
   1932—Remodeling: Frederick Brooke

One of the earliest of the Beaux-Arts houses on the Avenue, the Herbert Wadsworth house originally had a porte-cochere which passed through the middle of the first floor. Terra-cotta trim, as well as cut stone, embellishes the tan press brick which forms the body of the building.

9

WASHINGTON CLUB
(Patterson House)
15 Dupont Circle, N.W.
1902—Stanford White

Built for the publisher of the Washington *Times Herald,* this white marble Renaissance palazzo presents its own method of dealing with Washington's nonrectangular intersections.

10

EMBASSY OF IRAQ
(Boardman House)
1801 P Street, N.W.
1893—Hornblower and Marshall

One of the few, and one of the finest, remaining Richardsonian Romanesque Revival houses in the city.

11

BELMONT HOUSE
1618 New Hampshire Avenue, N.W.
1908 — Sanson, Trumbauer

A prow with Palladian motifs, this building gains much of its romance and strength from the direct, not to say head-on, approach to the problem of its triangular site. It was designed by a fashionable French architect who was especially imported for the job.

12

THOMAS NELSON PAGE HOUSE
1759 R Street, N.W.
1897 — McKim, Mead and White

The Page house, designed by Stanford White for the famous Southern author before the turn of the century, is a Federal Revival building — a departure from the Romanesque Revival and Queen Anne styles which were most popular with local architectural firms of the period.

13

WOMEN'S NATIONAL DEMOCRATIC CLUB
(Weeks House)
1526 New Hampshire Avenue, N.W.
1892—Harvey Page

A large cape of a roof—with an occasional raised eye-lid, drapes down over angular, turreted Roman brickwork.

A building of great and sympathetic personality, this house maintains a composed detachment on a street consisting almost exclusively of attached houses.

14

EURAM BUILDING
21 Dupont Circle
1970—Hartman-Cox, architects
            James Madison Cutts, structural engineer

A vigorous and dramatic structure, featuring a surprising open inner court, this contemporary office building is the most original addition to the Dupont Circle area since the end of the first decade of the twentieth century. Post-tensioned concrete beams span the length of the glazed facades, springing from masonry piers at the corners.

BLAINE MANSION
2000 Massachusetts Avenue, N.W.
1881—John Fraser

This is the mansion of James G. Blaine, the "Plumed Knight" of American politics and three-time unsuccessful presidential candidate. Dour and Victorian, it stands in disapproving contrast to its younger, more self-assured stone neighbors.

BEALE HOUSE
2012 Massachusetts Avenue, N.W.
1898—Glen Brown

The Beale House still stands, but its equally somber next-door neighbor to the east, the Litchfield House, was demolished a few years ago.

17

INDONESIAN EMBASSY
(Walsh-McLean House)
2020 Massachusetts Avenue, N.W.
1903—Henry Andersen

". . . it expresses the dreams my mother and father had when they were poor in Colorado."
—Evalyn Walsh McLean, *Father Struck it Rich*

A slab of gold ore built into the front porch proclaims the source of Thomas Walsh's fortune. Reputedly the most expensive house in Washington in its day, some sixty rooms and a vast stairhall lurk within.

18

THE PHILLIPS GALLERY
1600 21st Street, N.W.
1612 21st Street, N.W. (Annex)
1897—Hornblower and Marshall
1915—McKim, Mead and White
HOURS: 11 A.M. TO 6 P.M. TUESDAY THRU SATURDAY; 2 P.M.
TO 7 P.M. SUNDAY; 11 A.M. TO 10 P.M. MONDAY

In the quiet intimacy of this turn-of-the-century brownstone is found one of the great private art collections. The character of the old building does not carry over into the new wing.

19

SOCIETY OF THE CINCINNATI
(Lars Anderson House)
2118 Massachusetts Avenue, N.W.
1900—Little and Brown
HOURS: 2 P.M. TO 4 P.M. DAILY EXCEPT SUNDAYS AND
HOLIDAYS

A walled entrance court of great dignity distinguishes this house from its neighbors.

20

COSMOS CLUB
(Townsend House)
2121 Massachusetts Avenue, N.W.
1900—Carrère and Hastings
1958—Additions: Horace W. Peaslee

The client in this case was the wife of a railway magnate. The elaborate mansion was built around the shell of an older building, the Hillyer house, upon orders from Mrs. Townsend, who was superstitious about living in a totally new house.

SHERIDAN STATUE
Sheridan Circle and Massachusetts Avenue, N.W.
1909—Gutzon Borglum, sculptor

The pigeon-plagued general, reduced to the role of mounted policeman, directs traffic around the circle and on to "Embassy Row" from the city center. This is but one of many such intersections stemming from the radial overlay of avenues in L'Enfant's plan. Each seems to corral at least one hero on horseback.

TURKISH EMBASSY
(Everett House)
1603 23rd Street, N.W.
1914—George Oakley Totten

Although Totten is perhaps best known for his neo-Venetian Gothic work in the Meridian Hill area, this building and the nearby Pakistan Embassy are each in a different vein. Totten's versatility is particularly evident here in the strong, geometric juxtapositions on the south side.

23

BUFFALO BRIDGE
23rd and Q Streets, N.W.
1914—Glenn and Bedford Brown
A. P. Proctor, sculptor

This bridge is particularly impressive from a point where the massive battlements and great arches of the span can be seen.

24

CHINESE EMBASSY
(Fahnestock house)
2311 Massachusetts Avenue, N.W.
1909—Nathan C. Wyeth

Designed and detailed in the eighteenth-century French manner, this building occupies a key position in the harmonious row of buildings north of Sheridan Circle. Wyeth, a prominent and talented architect, practiced in Washington for nearly fifty years.

25

PAKISTAN EMBASSY
(Moran House)
2315 Massachusetts Avenue, N.W.
1908—George Oakley Totten

This building and its Chinese twin next door are by different architects. Because of the correspondence of material, however, mansard roofs, cornice lines, and pilasters, and sympathetic although not identical details, they read together as a unified composition on the street.

26

CAMEROON CHANCERY
(Hague house)
2344 Massachusetts Avenue, N.W.
1906—George Oakley Totten, Jr.

A limestone chateau which further demonstrates the versatility of Totten, who was able to work successfully in a number of eclectic styles. The romantic and bold massing and detailing are characteristic of his work. This building marks the western end of the great turn-of-the-century residences in the Beaux-Arts style along Massachusetts Avenue, which began with the Wilkins' house at 17th Street.

27

WOODROW WILSON HOUSE
(Henry P. Fairbanks house)
2340 S Street, N.W.
c.1915—Waddy B. Wood

President and Mrs. Wilson occupied this comfortable Georgian Revival house on S Street from the end of his last term as President, in 1921, until his death in 1924.

28

THE LOUISE HOME
2145 Decatur Place, N.W.
1901—Ogden Codman

Symmetrical flanking wings open on to raised gardens which in turn overlook the herringbone entrance drive. The stair to the left of the Home is one of the City's hidden treats.

L Connecticut Avenue

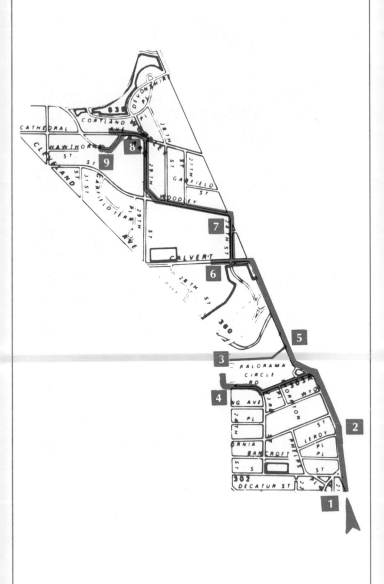

The character of this section of Connecticut Avenue, as it rises from the valley, has changed considerably since the end of World War II. A project called Crystal Heights, designed in 1948 by Frank Lloyd Wright, was the first indication of the developments that were to follow. At the top of the hill, the residential area of Kalorama is quietly defined by the valley of Rock Creek Park and Massachusetts Avenue beyond. Named after an 18th-century country house, Kalorama is one of the many residential areas in Washington whose tree-lined streets and architecture form distinct environments setting them uniquely apart from the sea of the city.

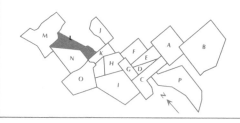

1

FRIENDS' MEETING HOUSE
2111 Florida Avenue, N.W.
1930—Walter H. Price

This simple stone structure recalls the Quaker buildings of rural Pennsylvania. The sundial on the upper terrace bears this inscription: "I mind the light, dost thou?"

2

LOTHROP MANSION
2001 Connecticut Avenue, N.W.
1901—Hornblower and Marshall

An unrivaled site, the prow formed by the intersection of Connecticut and Florida Avenues, is dominated by this house. The entrance court is to the rear.

3

THE LINDENS
2401 Kalorama Road, N.W.
1754—Robert Hooper (built in Danvers, Mass.)
1934—Moved to Washington, D.C.

This magnificent New England Georgian house was dismantled, moved in sections from its original site, and reconstructed here in 1934. It seems no less at home here than many of its eclectic neighbors.

4

DEVORE HOUSE
2000 24th Street, N.W.
1931—William L. Bottomley

Bottomley, that master of the new-old house, is here Gallic rather than James River Georgian, his better-known style. But, as usual, his rich detailing and balanced proportions carry the day.

5

WOODWARD APARTMENTS
2311 Connecticut Avenue, N.W.
1913—Harding and Upman

Crowned with a villa in the sky, this is one of the best of the many lavish apartment houses of its period in the immediate area. But, unlike some, it has not been altered by a contemporary remodeling.

6

SHOREHAM HOTEL
2500 Calvert Street, N.W.
1930—Joseph Abel

The drives, entrances and public spaces give a rich, varied, and expansive spatial experience. The Lobby, stepping down and opening out, presents an exciting view of Rock Creek Park as a surprising visual reward for entering the unpromising building.

SHERATON-PARK HOTEL
(Formerly Wardman-Park Hotel)
2660 Connecticut Avenue, N.W.
1918—Mesrobian-Wardman

SWISS EMBASSY
2900 Cathedral Avenue, N.W.
1959—William Lescaze

An unpretentious but well-crafted building which seems to reflect the thrifty virtues of its owners.

MARET SCHOOL
(Woodley House)
3000 Cathedral Avenue, N.W.
1800—Philip Barton Key, owner-builder

M Cleveland Park

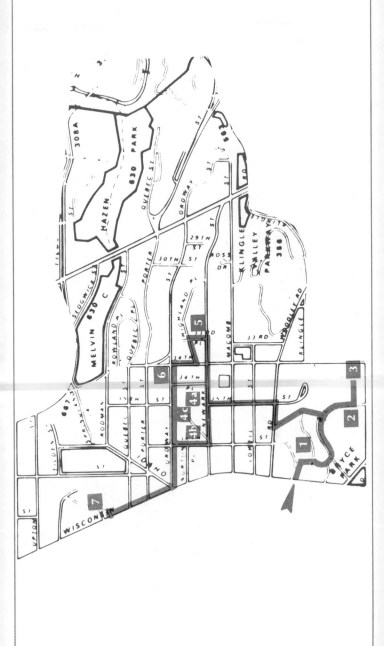

PRESIDENT CLEVELAND'S COUNTRY HOUSE.—DRAWN BY HUGHSON HAWLEY FROM THE ARCHITECTS' PLANS.

Named after President Cleveland's summer retreat, this charming section, with its great cathedral tower, is another example of the city's unique environments. Defined by well-marked geographical boundaries, this enclave is characterized by stucco architecture of the McKinley era, by high-crowned streets lined with elms and picket fences —along with striking examples of more contemporary talents.

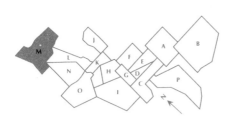

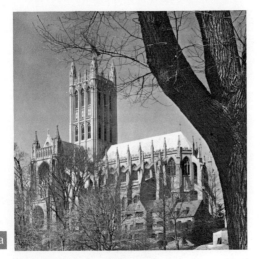

WASHINGTON CATHEDRAL
Massachusetts and Wisconsin Avenues, N.W.
1907—Vaughn, Bodley
c. 1917—Frohman, Robb and Little

Still under construction—and largely according to medieval structural principles—the Washington Cathedral proves that a Gothic interior, even though 600 years late, can still be an awesome experience. Radiant heating in the stone floor is one of the few concessions to modern life.

ST. ALBAN'S BRIDGE
35th and Garfield Street, N.W.
1961—Walter Dodd Ramberg

The donor of this bridge stipulated that the construction be of wood. It is notable not only for its design but also for the size of the members and the character of its joinery. An eighty-foot lathe was required to turn the large pine poles.

ST. ALBANS TENNIS CLUB
Pilgrim Road and Garfield Streets, N.W.
1970—Hartman and Cox
HOURS: 8 A.M. TO 6 P.M., APRIL THRU OCTOBER

A small and clever building of varied views and spaces whose cut-out order is at once elegant and peaceful.

ROSEDALE
3501 Newark Street, N.W.
1793—Uriah Forrest, owner-builder

A delightful farmhouse in the city, originally built as a summer retreat by General Uriah Forrest. Within a few years, however, the General moved from Georgetown to live in Rosedale the year 'round.

WALDRON FAULKNER HOUSE
3415 36th Street, N.W.
1937—Waldron Faulkner, FAIA
Private residence

A classically proportioned and symmetrical house of its time that addresses itself to the street with the reserve of a scholar.

WINTHROP FAULKNER HOUSE
3530 Ordway Street, N.W.
1964—Winthrop Faulkner

Pictured is the first of a pair of handsome contemporary houses by the same architect-client.

5

HIGHLAND PLACE
N.W. off 34th Street

On this street lined with tall gnarled oaks is gathered a collection of houses that are typically nineteenth-century American. The architecture of the front porch, at once romantic and picturesque, evokes nostaligic sounds of childrens' laughter across the backyards, player pianos and the unmistakable bang of the screen door.

6

SLAYTON HOUSE
3411 Ordway Street, N.W.
1962—I. M. Pei

7

FRIENDS' SCHOOL ADMINISTRATION BUILDING
(The Highlands)
3825 Wisconsin Avenue, N.W.
1816–1822—Charles Joseph Nourse, owner-builder

One of the few stone houses in the area from the early nineteenth century. The Highlands' land once adjoined that of Rosedale. Square stone columns on the western front are comparatively recent.

N Massachusetts Avenue

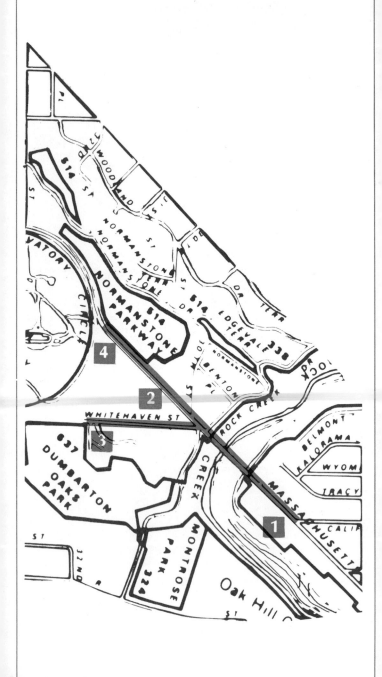

This is the longest of the avenues, cutting a great diagonal swath across the heart of the city from southeast to northwest. It is at its best from Dupont Circle on. The color, pageantry and pride of the nations constitute the character of Embassy Row.

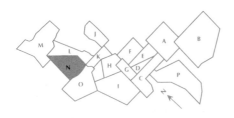

JAPANESE EMBASSY (Tea House)
2521 Massachusetts Avenue, N.W.
1958—Delano and Aldrich (Embassy)
        Nahiko Emori (Tea House)

The simple pedimented facade behind the pole fence and graveled drive makes this a colonial outpost among the architectural stage sets along this strip of Massachusetts Avenue. In the garden behind is an authentic Japanese tea house.

BRAZILIAN EMBASSY
(McCormick house)
3000 Massachusetts Avenue, N.W.
1931—John Russell Pope (embassy)
1973—Olavo de Campos (chancery)

The Pope palazzo formula—here with recessed entrance —derived from the Palazzo Massimi alle Colonne in Rome by Peruzzi. To the north of the residence the dark glass facade enclosing the chancery is suspended from roof trusses, which cantilever out beyond the interior columns.

DANISH EMBASSY
3200 Whitehaven Street, N.W.
1959—Wilhelm Lauritzen

The building is cool, white, and almost crystalline against the wooded hill, but much of its positive effect is lost when seen over a sea of polychromed tin. The entrance is a parking lot.

BRITISH EMBASSY
3100 Massachusetts Avenue, N.W.
1931—Sir Edward Lutyens

". . . there's some corner of a foreign field that is forever England."

—Rupert Brooke

Almost hidden behind the winged symmetry of the forecourt is the picturesque and skillful massing characteristic of Lutyens' work.

O Georgetown

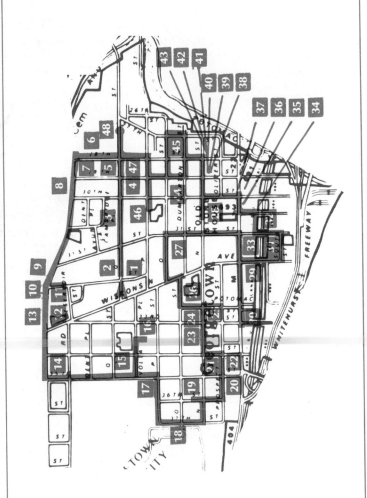

Georgetown, older than the city of which it is now a part, prides itself on its antiquity and its eighteenth century atmosphere. The original town, laid out in 1751, consisted of about sixty acres, the land lying between the river and a line south of N Street, bounded by what is now 30th Street on the east and the grounds of Georgetown University on the west. There are still a number of buildings within these bounds that date from Georgetown's first half century, but most of the fine old houses that give the streets their special quality and charm are from the period after 1800.

The growth of the Federal Government and the consequent increase in population has in more recent years brought about the re-discovery of Georgetown as a choice place to live, convenient to the heart of the city, and government officials and members of Congress once more, like their counterparts in 1800, seek houses in Georgetown. The citizens have obtained legislation to ensure the preservation of the architectural character of their town, and under the provisions of the Georgetown Act plans for additions or restoration of old buildings, as well as plans for new construction, have to be approved by an appointed commission. Unfortunately, the legislation does not restrict the destruction of old buildings, many of which have been lost in recent years. In the main, however, Georgetown has managed to retain its unique quality, quite different from other parts of Washington, contributing interest and variety to the urban scene in the nation's capital.

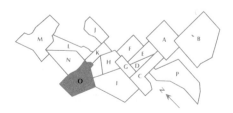

1

EPISCOPAL HOME
(Bowie-Sevier House)
3124 Q Street, N.W.
1805—Washington Bowie, owner-builder
1957—Horace Peaslee, architect for additions, alterations

Only the central portion of this house is original. The estate once embraced the entire block.

2

TUDOR PLACE
1644 31st Street, N.W.
1815—Dr. William Thornton

This house—perhaps Thornton's masterpiece—represents a significant break with the earlier, Georgian architecture of the preceding century. The Bowie-Sevier house, directly across Q Street, offers a convenient comparison.

3

COOKE'S ROW
3007–3029 Q Street, N.W.
1868—Starkweather and Plowman

This magnificent run of detached Victorian houses points out the fallacy of assuming that Georgetown owes all of its character and charm to its far-from-uniform Federal row buildings.

4

FRANCIS DODGE HOUSE
1517 30th Street, N.W.
1852—A. J. Downing and Calvert Vaux

Designed and built at the same time as the Robert Dodge house at the corner of Q and 28th Streets, this building retains the Italianate character of the original design. Both houses were described in Vaux's book *Villas and Cottages*, published in 1857.

5

R. E. LEE HOUSE
2813 Q Street, N.W.
1959—Hugh Newell Jacobsen

The original structure was only the western half of this expanded house. Vertical proportions of the new sash and other contemporary exterior details are in complete harmony with the architectural character of the older elements of the building, and with its neighbors—a demonstration that proved to Georgetown and its aesthetic rear guard that the twentieth century wasn't incompatible with the nineteenth.

6

EVERMAY
1628 28th Street, N.W.
1801—Nicholas King,
     Nicholas Hedges, builder

Samuel Davidson, the original owner, issued a notice saying: "I beg and pray of all my neighbors to avoid Evermay as they would a den of devils, or rattlesnakes, and thereby save themselves and me much vexation and trouble."

Those who dared to venture past the gate discovered a great house on what may be the most magnificent residential site in the city, a corner bluff overlooking Rock Creek Park and Oak Hill Cemetery.

MACKALL SQUARE
1633 29th Street, N.W.
1820—Benjamin Mackall, owner-builder

OAK HILL CEMETERY GATEHOUSE
30th and R Streets, N.W.
1850—de la Roche
Gift of W. W. Corcoran

OAK HILL CHAPEL
1850—James Renwick

Near the entrance of Oak Hill Cemetery is this Gothic Revival chapel, a paperweight in stone.

When compared with Renwick's Smithsonian Institution and St. Patrick's Cathedral in New York, its simple, restrained character and charm point up this architect's great range and versatility.

8c

VAN NESS MAUSOLEUM
Oak Hill Cemetery
30th and R Streets, N.W.
1833—George Hadfield

Based on the Temple of Vesta in Rome, this tomb stands among the trees on the eastern heights of the cemetery hill. The architect is better known for the Old City Hall and Arlington.

9

LOVERS LANE
Montrose Park
3001 R Street, N.W. and Lovers Lane

Lovers Lane, as it is officially known, separates Montrose Park—an English Romantic landscape—from Dumbarton Oaks, a formal Renaissance garden.

10a

DUMBARTON OAKS
3101 R Street, N.W.
1801—William Hammond Dorsey, owner-builder
1822—Frederich Brooke (alterations)
Music Room and Residences, Lawrence White
Extensive Gardens, Mrs. Beatrice Farrand

Although Dumbarton Oaks has been so altered and extended that little of the original architecture is visible, is has remained a building of great character. It is the formal, terraced gardens, however, which are the particular attraction here. They have suffered recent modifications.

10b

PRE-COLUMBIAN MUSEUM
Dumbarton Oaks
1703 32nd Street, N.W.
1963—Philip Johnson

"It seems I cannot but be classically inspired; symmetry, order, clarity above all. I cannot throw around cardboard boxes, or make a pseudo-functional arrangement of air-conditioning ducts into a trouvé-d type of design."
—Philip Johnson, Perspecta 7

The plan is composed of nine interlocking circles of columns; eight are domed; the ninth, the center, is open to a pool. Teak, two types of marble, bronze, and glass are the dominant materials.

ANDRE DE LIMUR HOUSE
3224 R Street, N.W.
1948—Theodore Dominick

SCOTT-GRANT HOUSE
3238 R Street, N.W.
1858—A. V. Scott, owner-builder

DOUGALL HOUSE
3259 R Street, N.W.
1854—Adams and Haskins

MACKALL-WORTHINGTON HOUSE
1686 34th Street, N.W.
1820—Leonard Mackall, owner-builder

Built in that part of Georgetown once known as "The Heights," the Leonard Mackall house was once on the outskirts of town and, until recently, dominated the block on which it stands.

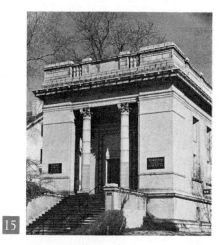

VOLTA BUREAU
1537 35th Street, N.W.
1893—Peabody and Stearns

This is the headquarters of the American Association to Promote the Teaching of Speech to the Deaf, an organization established by Alexander Graham Bell with the $10,000 Volta prize awarded him for the invention of the telephone. It is pure temple on the front only; the other elevations admit its use as an office building.

POMANDER WALK
Volta Place, between 33rd and 34th Streets, N.W.
1885

Within the last thirty years this alley has changed from a slum to a small attractive enclave with tiny houses of rare charm.

CONVENT OF THE VISITATION
35th and P Streets, N.W.
1825—Joseph Picot de Clorivière
1857—Monastery
1874—Academy Building, Norris G. Starkweather

Three different architectural styles are combined here in one continuous strip. They build up from austere Federal to ornate Victorian, via an odd combination of Gothic-Classic.

**GEORGETOWN UNIVERSITY
HEALY BUILDING
1879—Smithmeyer and Pelz**

Giving a touch of the Rhine to the Potomac, this baronial Jesuit fortress was designed, rather surprisingly, by the ambidextrous architects of the Library of Congress. It completely dominates the older Federal and neo-Classic buildings directly behind.

**GEORGETOWN UNIVERSITY LIBRARY
(Joseph Mark Lauinger Memorial Library)
1970—John Carl Warnecke & Associates**

The broken massing and warm gray color of this exposed-concrete structure do not detract from the dominance of the Healy building on the quadrangle, and its relatively low profile maintains the romantic view of the old tower from across the river.

18c

GEORGETOWN UNIVERSITY
OLD NORTH BUILDING
1793–1795

Earliest of the university buildings, Old North is similar to other simple, collegiate, brick, Georgian or Federal structures. Daniel Rieff, in *Washington Architecture, 1791–1861,* also points out its similarity to the residential block in southwest Washington known as Wheat Row (Tour P.2).

19

HOLY TRINITY PARISH
36th Street, between N and O Streets, N.W.
1794—Original church (now Convent of Mercy)
3513 N Street, N.W.
1851—Present Church (illustrated)
1869—Rectory—3514 O Street, N.W.
Francis Stanton, architect

The original church was the first building for public Catholic worship in the District of Columbia. In 1851 it was replaced by the simple, handsome Greco-Roman Revival church which stands in the middle of the block on 36th Street. During the Civil War it served as a hospital for Union troops.

PROSPECT HOUSE
3508 Prospect Street, N.W.
1788—James Maccubbin Lingan, owner-builder

The view from this house to the south down the Potomac is the prospect that provides the name.

"QUALITY HILL"
3425 Prospect Street, N.W.
1798—John Thomson Mason, owner-builder

The name of this house may have been first attached to the immediate neighborhood because of the many fine houses situated here.

22

BENJAMIN STODDERT HOUSE
(Halcyon House)
3400 Prospect Avenue, N.W.
1787—Benjamin Stoddert, owner-builder

Benjamin Stoddert, the country's first Secretary of the Navy, built Halcyon House "after the manner of some of the elegant houses I have seen in Philadelphia." While the south facade is largely original, the north is heavily if romantically disfigured.

23

COX'S ROW
3327–3339 N Street, N.W.
1817—John Cox, owner-builder

"A house that has character stands a good chance of growing more valuable as it grows older, while a house in the prevailing mode, whatever that mode may be, is soon out of fashion, stale, and unprofitable."

—Frank Lloyd Wright
The Architectural Record, March, 1908

An unusual aspect of this row is its setback from the street. Of these fine houses, three show traces of Victorian remodeling. However, having survived the changes of taste intact, the two end houses stand, with their leaden swags and arched doorways, as fine examples of Federal architecture.

SMITH ROW
3255–3263 N Street, N.W.
1815—Walter and Clement Smith, owner-builders

This full block of Federal houses is an object lesson in minor variations on a simple, consistent theme. Comparison with Cox's Row in the adjoining block will emphasize the raised and, in some of the houses, larger-windowed parlor floors here.

BODISCO HOUSE
3222 O Street, N.W.
1815—Clement Smith, owner-builder

ST. JOHN'S CHURCH
Potomac and O Streets, N.W.
1804—Dr. William Thornton
1870—Starkweather and Plowman

Thornton, architect of the Capitol, Tudor Place and Octagon House, provided the architectural inspiration, if not the drawings, for this church. However, his ideas were not closely followed during the original construction, and the building has been greatly modified during later years.

CHRIST CHURCH
31st and O Streets, N.W.
1885—Henry Laws

This is almost a Gothic cathedral in miniature. The scale has been so reduced that the elements seem small next to the neighboring houses. Ranks of sharp gables, the precarious tower, and the sepia interior move this building well beyond the range of mere eclecticism. Since most of the neighboring houses are from the same period, the church is seen against an appropriate background.

28

WASHINGTON POST OFFICE, GEORGETOWN BRANCH
(Custom House)
1221 31st Street, N.W.
1857—Ammi B. Young

A native of New Hampshire, Young had also designed the Vermont State Capitol (1832) and the Boston Custom House (1837) before coming to Washington where he was appointed Supervising Architect of the Treasury in 1852. Talbot Hamlin, in *Greek Revival Architecture in America,* writes of the building as "the best of these Italianate Federal buildings."

29

CITY TAVERN
3206 M Street, N.W.
1796
1961—Macomber and Peter, reconstruction

Some of the upper-floor rooms of this late-eighteenth-century tavern (reconstructed and readapted for the use of a private club) are intact and restored. The lower floor and brick facade are new. Originally, carriages rode through a larger arched opening at the street to a courtyard in the rear.

30

THE GEORGETOWN MARKET
3276 M Street, N.W.
1865—

This forlorn-looking building, used as a wholesale warehouse since 1935, deserves rehabilitation and reuse for its original purpose—that of a market. The site was used as a public market from 1795 when the ground was deeded to the city "for the use of the market aforesaid forever, and for no other use, interest or purpose whatsoever."

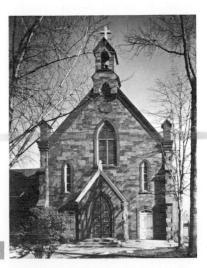

31

GRACE CHURCH
South Street at Wisconsin Avenue, N.W.
1866

"Let not Ambition mock their useful toil.
Their homely joys, and destiny obscure. . . ."
—Thomas Gray, *Elegy Written in a Country Churchyard*

Set back on its raised courtyard, this small and humble Gothic Revival church seems unaffected by the passage of time. The interior, still intact, has the character of a 19th-century stage set. It was originally built as a mission church for boatmen on the nearby Chesapeake and Ohio Canal.

32a

CHESAPEAKE & OHIO CANAL

32b

Warehouses
Between Potomac Street and Jefferson Place
1823 and after

Closed commercially in 1923 and now largely dry, the canal once ran 186 miles from Cumberland, Maryland, to Alexandria, Virginia, crossing the Potomac on the Viaduct Bridge.

It was never the commercial success its sponsors, including George Washington, had envisioned. The railway line running parallel—founded on the same day in 1823— soon proved a faster and cheaper shipping route.

The Canal now attracts hikers, bicyclists, canoeists and fishermen. A long Park Service barge, "The Canal Clipper," serves as a reminder of other days.

The Functional Tradition warehouses and Towpath Lane houses where the canal slips quietly into Georgetown are of particular architectural interest.

33

CANAL SQUARE
1054 31st Street, N.W.
1971—Arthur Cotton More & Associates

An old canalside warehouse was incorporated into this lively contemporary center for specialty shops, restaurants and offices.

34

POTOMAC MASONIC LODGE #75
1058 Jefferson Street, N.W.
1810

This Lodge officiated at the laying of the cornerstone of the Capitol. Now remodeled as a planner/architect's office, this building ties down one corner of the city's most romantic single block. Thomas Jefferson's house before he was President once stood on the east side of the street.

OLD STONE HOUSE
3051 M Street, N.W.
c. 1766—Christopher Layhman, builder

Various legends hold that this was Washington's engineering headquarters and L'Enfant's headquarters. Although the traditional stories have been discredited, it is the oldest remaining building in the District.

LOUGHBORO-PATTERSON HOUSE
3039–3041 M Street, N.W.
1801–1806
Restored 1963—Macomber and Peter

A careful and authentic restoration to the Federal facades on a street that seems, at times, unsure as to which end of the 19th Century it belongs. Here, Federal and Victorian buildings alternate and confront each other, often to their mutual advantage.

HISTORIC GEORGETOWN
(Thomas Sim Lee Corner)
3001–3009 M Street, N.W.
1794, 1810
Restored c. 1955 — Howe, Foster and Snyder

The two end houses on the corner of Thirtieth and M Streets have been called "The finest examples of late pre-revolutionary buildings in the town." Research reveals that they were originally one building and that the street level was cut down. What is now the shop level was once the below-grade basement.

LAIRD-DUNLOP HOUSE
3014 N Street, N.W.
1799 — Attributed to William Lovering, architect-builder

The rounded vault of the entrance porch is picked up in the brick arches of the windows alongside. These windows relate the house to the Law or "Honeymoon House," in the Southwest Renewal area.

RIGGS-RILEY HOUSE
3038 N Street, N.W.
1816—Romulus Riggs, owner-builder

This is a fine, balanced example of the small Georgetown Federal house. It is an architectural concept whose requisite subtleties almost invariably escape the "neo-Federal" builders—with near disastrous results.

WHEATLEY HOUSES
3041–3043 N Street, N.W.
1859—Francis Wheatley, builder

This mirror-image pair of Victorian variations on the flat-facade town house theme is marked by sinuous and organic window heads, and the strong rhythm of the cornice. The tall, narrow windows of the parlor floor are well above street level, allowing them to be dropped to the floor and still maintain some semblance of privacy.

FOXALL HOUSE
2908 N Street, N.W.
c. 1820—Henry Foxall, owner-builder

The small, wall-enclosed, two-dormer over three-bay portion is the original house. Henry Foxall was the owner of a prosperous foundry on the western outskirts of Georgetown.

DECATUR HOUSE
2812 N Street, N.W.
1813—J. S. Williams

According to legend, this is the house to which Commodore Decatur's widow moved after his tragic duel.

43

GANNT-WILLIAMS HOUSE
2806 N Street, N.W.
1817

This house is distinguished by slightly vertical emphasis, wedged lintels and elaborate dormers.

44

MT. ZION UNITED METHODIST CHURCH
1334 29th Street, N.W.
1876–1884

Reputedly the oldest Negro church in the District of Columbia, their records go back to 1830, but the congregation was organized and built their first church on 27th Street above P Street about 1814. Before the Civil War it was known as a station of the underground railroad.

45

TRENTMAN HOUSE
1350 27th Street, N.W.
1968—Hugh Newell Jacobsen

A thoroughly modern house that asserts its own quality of design, the Trentman house fits in, nevertheless, with its traditional Georgetown neighbors through careful attention to form, scale, proportion and use of materials.

46

LINTHICUM HOUSE
3019 P Street, N.W.
1829—Edward Linthicum, owner-builder

Edward Linthicum moved from this house into Dumbarton Oaks. The rich, noticeably wide doorway, hard against the sidewalk is the notable feature here.

47

MILLER HOUSE
1524 28th Street, N.W.
1840—Benjamin Miller, owner-builder

Federal format in wood rather than brick, this house seems more New England than Southern. The dominant entrance porch is, however, a turn toward the Greek Revival.

48

SOCIETY OF COLONIAL DAMES
(Dumbarton House)
2715 Q Street, N.W.
c. 1800
1805—Benjamin H. Latrobe (Remodeled)
1915—(Moved to present site)

One of the oldest of the large Georgian houses in Georgetown, Dumbarton House was remodeled by Latrobe, who added the rear bays.

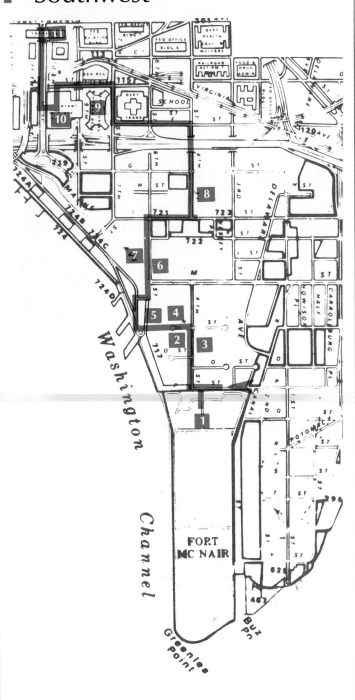

This area has been called the finest urban renewal effort in the country, and buildings are still being added. The 552-acre renewal tract runs the gamut of building types, all arranged to an over-all plan. With the exception of the few historical town houses selected for preservation, and some commercial buildings along the waterfront, almost all of the architecture is brand-new. This is Washington's showplace of contemporary building, and perhaps it will in the future constitute an outdoor museum of the architectural clichés of the two decades following World War II.

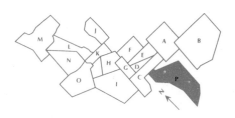

FORT McNAIR
Fourth and P Streets, S.W.

Situated on Greenleaf Point, which is formed by the junction of the Potomac Channel and the Anacostia River, Fort McNair is blessed with one of the most beautiful sites in the city. At the apex is the Army War College, tough and stern Beaux-Arts. The officers' houses, idyllic along the breakwater of the Washington Channel, are a special Washington unto themselves.

ARMY WAR COLLEGE
1908—McKim, Mead and White

ENLISTED MEN'S HOUSING

WHEAT ROW—HARBOUR SQUARE
1313-1321 4th Street, S.W.
1793—attributed to William Lovering
1966—Chloethiel Woodard Smith Associates

This group of Federal houses was selected to be saved, renovated and integrated with the new architecture of the Renewal Area.

In 1966, together with the Duncanson-Cranch House and the Washington-Lewis House, around the corner on N Street, they were incorporated in the construction of the Harbour Square complex.

RIVER PARK APARTMENTS
4th and Delaware Avenue, S.W.
1962—Charles M. Goodman Associates

The apartment building here serves as a boundary wall to separate the adjoining townhouses from public housing beyond. Vaulted roofs and aluminum screens are distinctive elements in the residential courts around which the townhouses have been grouped.

TIBER ISLAND
429 N Street, S.W.
1965—Keyes, Lethbridge and Condon

This pinwheel scheme and the adjoining Carrollsburg Square development east of 4th Street were winners of two successive Redevelopment Land Agency architectural competitions. Close juxtaposition of apartment towers and townhouses, covered parking under a central plaza, and a carefully limited range of materials and colors are three of the more important aspects.

5

LAW HOUSE
6th and N Streets, S.W.
1796—Attributed to William Lovering

Called "Honeymoon House" because Thomas and Eliza Law spent their honeymoon here, this was one of the new city's first speculative houses. It is now a community house for the residents of Tiber Island. Law, an influential businessman, subsequently occupied three other houses in Washington.

6

TOWN CENTER PLAZA
1100 block of 3rd Street, S.W.
1100 block of 6th Street, S.W.
1961–1962—I. M. Pei Associates
1972—Chloethiel Woodward Smith Associates

Built in two stages, with an adjoining shopping center, the original apartment complex, unlike others in the area, had neither townhouses nor balconies. The simple, classic siting was complemented by the tight-skinned buildings themselves. The larger commercial center, built ten years later, fills out the block.

7a

ARENA STAGE
6th and M Streets, S.W.
1961—Harry Weese & Associates
1970—Harry Weese & Associates, addition

"What of architectural beauty I now see, I know has grad-ually grown from within outward, out of the necessities and character of the indweller . . ."
—Henry David Thoreau, *Walden,* 1854

The strength of this building is on many levels: in the clear division and appropriate expression of usage, in the imaginative structure and details, and in the sequence of space from entrance to performance. Moreover, it is a building which need not apologize for its low cost.

The Kreeger Theater, supplementing the earlier "theater-in-the-round," is a fan-shaped structure with a thrust stage, seating about 500 persons.

7b

8

CAPITOL PARK APARTMENTS (South)
800 4th Street, S.W.
1958—Satterlee and Smith

This was the first of a group of similar buildings. It is characterized by the architects' deliberate attempt to provide scale, intimacy, and variety in a large apartment building.

9

DEPARTMENT OF HOUSING
AND URBAN DEVELOPMENT
451 7th Street, S.W.
1968—Marcel Breuer & Associates
          Nolen, Swinburne & Associates

The curved form and deeply modeled window panels are characteristic of Breuer's work. Dark stone facing on the projecting end walls provides a contrast to the light, precast-concrete facades.

L'ENFANT PLAZA
L'Enfant Plaza, S.W.
1965 — I. M. Pei & Partners
    Araldo Cossutta, design partner
1970–1973 — Hotel and West Office Building
    Vlastimil Koubek

An outgrowth of the Zeckendorf-Pei plan for southwest Washington, L'Enfant Plaza is the termination of the 10th Street Mall from Independence Avenue. The first two office buildings, north and south of the plaza, are a sophisticated example *in situ* concrete design, the mechanical and electrical systems being integrated with the exposed coffered ceilings. The two subsequent buildings, east and west of the plaza, are faced with precast panels.

FORRESTAL BUILDING
Independence Avenue and 10th Street, S.W.
1970 — Curtis and Davis
    Fordyce and Hamby Associates
    Frank Grad & Sons

Three buildings make up this group — the longest bridging the entrance to the 10th Street Mall. All are neo-heroic in scale — a new generation of Federal formalism, but a product of the same planning mentality that produced the Federal Triangle in the nineteen-twenties.

Q D.C. Places

THE POTOMAC AT THE LITTLE FALLS

Washington is a square—ten miles on each side—with one corner removed. This was given back to Virginia. L'Enfant located the Capitol in the center, but the pattern of growth, like that of any other city, spasmodic and uneven, has shifted the real center to the northwest. As a result, a number of significant structures have been left high and dry.

WASHINGTON CANOE CLUB
West end of K Street, N.W., above Key Bridge
c. 1890

A turn-of-the century Shingle-style building which recalls to mind the heavy-roofed, turreted forms of summerhouse architecture of the period. The view of the Canoe Club from across the river, a romantic counterpoint at the water's edge to the towers of Healy on the horizon, is a favorite of many Washingtonians.

GEORGETOWN UNIVERSITY HOSPITAL PARKING STRUCTURE
3800 Reservoir Road, N.W.
1967—Mariani & Associates

This building deserves notice as a generally successful solution to a very difficult problem—a large parking facility (530 cars) in close juxtaposition to other buildings. Partially submerged in the ground, the structure is capped with planting at its edge and a landscaped plaza, hiding the parked cars from the street-level view.

3

GERMAN EMBASSY CHANCERY
4645 Reservoir Road, N.W.
1964 — Egon Eiermann

"The architect is not bound to exhibit structure . . . nevertheless, that building will generally be the noblest, which to an intelligent eye discovers the great secrets of its structure . . . although from a careless observer they may be concealed."
— John Ruskin, *The Seven Lamps of Architecture*
The Chancery serves both as a closing wall along the edge of the site and as a link between the Embassy Residence on Foxhall Road above and the business entrance on Reservoir Road below. By stepping down at each end, the building drops close to the scale of the nearby houses.

4

BENDING LANE HOUSES
4800 Reservoir Road and Bending Lane, N.W.
1960 — Grosvenor Chapman

Thoughtful planting and the screening of yards and approaches provide both interest and privacy for these houses. They form one of the city's few enclaves of contemporary building.

5a

FLORENCE HOLLIS HAND CHAPEL
MOUNT VERNON COLLEGE
2100 Foxhall Road, N.W.
1970—Hartman-Cox
HOURS: 10 A.M. TO 5 P.M. SCHOOL DAYS, OR INQUIRE AT
GATEHOUSE

This highly imaginative college chapel addresses itself
outside to the scale of the campus and its residential neighborhood, yet creates an impressive interior volume by
taking advantage of the hillside on which it is sited. The
stepped clerestory roof is a brave detail that works, for the
overall intensity of interior light is high enough to avoid
uncomfortable contrasts.

5b

DORMITORY, MOUNT VERNON COLLEGE
2100 Foxhall Road, N.W.
1971—Hartman-Cox
Not open to the public

A confidently executed and carefully detailed expression
of the materials used, the sweeping lines of this building
produce an eloquent solution to a complex problem. Each
room within shares a view of woodland and the river beyond.

6

DAVID LLOYD
KREEGER HOUSE
2401 Foxhall Road, N.W.
1967 — Philip Johnson & Richard Foster
Private residence

A Roman villa designed to house the owner's extensive collection of art, this house is a rare contemporary example of the client as a patron of architecture rather than as a consumer of the products of the shelter industry.

7

BELGIAN EMBASSY
2300 Foxhall Road, N.W.
1931 — Horace Trumbauer

"There was music from my neighbor's house through the summer nights. In his blue gardens men and girls came and went like moths among the whisperings and the champagne stars."

—F. Scott Fitzgerald, *The Great Gatsby, 1925*

Washington is a city in which mansions are almost common, but it has few which can match the restrained elegance found here. The Hotel de Charolais in Paris supplied the front facade.

8

ROCK CREEK PARK
1890

Rock Creek Park, the largest part in the National Capital Parks system, at some 1800 acres, is but one segment of the chain of parks lining the creek. It abuts the National Zoological Park on the south; Dumbarton Oaks Park, Montrose Park, Oak Hill Cemetary, and Rock Creek Parkway follow in sequence to the Potomac.

Originally acquired in 1890, Rock Creek was enlarged in 1924, to preserve the tributaries as well. One of the city's most significant natural features, Rock Creek makes a wild green swath through the city, defining boundaries on its way. In wildness and size, the park is unmatched by that of any other city in America—if not in the world.

9

NATIONAL ZOOLOGICAL PARK
3100 Connecticut Avenue, N.W.
Monkey House
1907—Hornblower & Marshall
HOURS: 9 A.M. TO 4:30 P.M. (FALL AND WINTER)
9 A.M. TO 6 P.M. (SPRING AND SUMMER)

The zoo is a collection of romantic buildings, as well as of animals, the best of which evoke their purpose. A noteworthy example is the Monkey House, clad in a moss-like stone and topped with a purple and green tile roof, with bear cub, bobcat and fox finials.

10

STABLE, NATIONAL PARK SERVICE
(Rock Creek Park Horse Center)
Glover & Military Roads, N.W.
1972 — Hartman-Cox
HOURS: 9 A.M. TO 5 P.M., TUESDAY THRU SUNDAY

A stable that is detailed in the board and batten tradition, enlivened by a variety of openings, both in size and form. The geometry of the roof form, cutaway to meet the requirements of plan, is the unifying element of the composition.

11

CALVERT STREET BRIDGE
Calvert Street, N.W. over Rock Creek
1935 — Paul P. Cret

This handsome structure, with its wide sidewalks and graceful concrete arches, crosses the Rock Creek Valley which lies more than 120 feet below. The four pylons of the bridge, at each corner of its approaches, are decorated with sculpture symbolizing four media of travel: air, rail, water and highway. It is but one of several notable bridges in the area.

LINNEAN HILL
3545 Williamsburg Lane, N.W.
1832—No architect's name available

Built by mill owner Jacob Pierce upon what is perhaps the best site in the city, this stone house was restored for office use by the Park Service in 1935. A rather clumsy late-nineteenth-century addition at the entry is overshadowed by the graceful porch on the south.

PIERCE MILL
2311 Tilden Street, N.W.
1810

This is the one mill remaining of the eight that were formerly in Rock Creek Park. It is unusual in being "undershot," i.e., the water turns the wheel from below.

BERLINER HOUSE
2841 Tilden Street, N.W.
1958—Charles Goodman

15

LE DROIT PARK
Florida & Rhode Island Avenues, N.W.
1873–1877—James McGill

Many of the houses in this neighborhood were designed and built by James McGill, a nineteenth-century entrepreneur, in the romantic styles of the period. Gothic cottage, Italian villa and Second Empire shingle—they were built on speculation a century ago, but still continue to contribute to the architectural interest and variety of the city. Le Droit Park has long been a center of the cultural and social life associated with nearby Howard University.

16

HOWARD HALL
(Howard University)
607 Howard Place, N.W.
1867—No architect's name available
HOURS 8 A.M. TO 5 P.M., MONDAY THRU FRIDAY

A post-Civil War example of the residential French Renaissance style, this was the home of General Oliver O. Howard, founder of Howard University. Neglected and in need of restoration, the house still dominates the hill like a shabby but genteel dowager.

17

OLD SOLDIERS' HOME
3700 block of North Capitol Street, N.W.
(Rock Creek Church Road at Upshur Street, N.W.)
1843—Anderson Cottage
1852—B. S. Alexander and others (Sherman Building)

Founded in 1851, this is the oldest soldiers' home in the United States. Nestled among the Norman Gothic ramparts is the stuccoed Anderson Cottage. The first building of the Home, it was used by various Presidents, including Lincoln, as a summer White House.

18

FRANCISCAN MONASTERY
1400 Quincy Street, N.E.
1899—Aristides Leonori
HOURS: 8 A.M. TO 5 P.M. ALL YEAR

A highly romantic evocation of fourteenth-century Italy. Nearby on Michigan Avenue, surrounded by the campus of Catholic University, is the Shrine of the Immaculate Conception, a massive Byzantine basilica which commenced construction in 1920 and which stands today as one of the largest church edifices in the United States. Also worthy of note is the Chapel of Notre Dame at the north side of the Trinity College grounds, Michigan Avenue and Harewood Road.

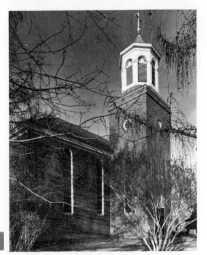

ST. PAUL'S CHURCH
c. 1772
ROCK CREEK CEMETERY
Webster and 3rd Streets, N.W.
1719

The original chapel was the first church in the District.
The present church is a restoration of 1921.

ROCK CREEK CEMETERY
ADAMS MEMORIAL, "GRIEF"
1890—Augustus St. Gaudens (statue)
Stanford White (base)

"The interest of the figure was not in its meaning, but in
the response of the observer."
—Henry Adams, *The Education of Henry Adams, 1907*
Hidden in a grove of holly and evergreen is Henry Adams'
memorial to his wife, a suicide.

20

SURSUM CORDA
M and First Streets, N.W.
1969 — Collins & Kronstadt-Leahy, Hogan, Collins

The placement of buildings, with their walled gardens and heavy textures, forms spaces and vistas which are truly urban, yet informal enough to establish a feeling of warmth — a quality rarely achieved in low-income housing.

21

GALLAUDET COLLEGE
7th and Florida Avenue, N.E.
1867 — Vaux and Withers (President's House)
1874–1877 — Withers (College Hall)
Daniel Chester French (statue)

The grounds of this small school and college for the education of the deaf were laid out in 1866 by the landscape architect of New York's Central Park, Frederick Law Olmsted, Sr. The original Victorian-Gothic buildings are in complete harmony with the studied informality of Olmsted's planning.

22

NATIONAL ARBORETUM
24th and R Streets, N.E.
Administration Building
1963—Deigert & Yerkes Associates
HOURS: 8 A.M. TO 5 P.M., MONDAY THRU FRIDAY
GROUNDS: 8 A.M. TO 7 P.M., APRIL THRU OCTOBER
    10 A.M. TO 7 P.M., WEEKENDS
    8 A.M. TO 5 P.M., NOVEMBER THRU MARCH
    10 A.M. TO 5 P.M., WEEKENDS

Pools and fountains surround this romantic, yet formal building that adjoins the extensive gardens of the Arboretum. The administration building contains an exhibit hall and auditorium besides offices which oversee the 415 acres of trees, flowering shrubs, gazebos and garden pavilions.

23

CEDAR HILL
(Frederick Douglass House)
14th and W Streets, S. E.
1859—architect unknown
HOURS: 9 A.M. TO 4 P.M., WEEKDAYS
    10 A.M. TO 5 P.M., SUNDAYS
    CLOSED CHRISTMAS DAY ONLY

"Born of the sun they traveled a short while towards the sun, And left the vivid air signed with their honor."
—Stephen Spender

This mid-nineteenth-century house was the home of Frederick Douglass, author, abolitionist and antislavery editor. Recently restored by the National Park Service, it graces a hill overlooking the city from beyond the Anacostia River.

24

FAIRFAX VILLAGE RECREATION CENTER
41st Street and Alabama Avenue, S. E.
1969—Hartman-Cox
HOURS: 12:30 TO 9:00 P.M., EXCEPT SATURDAY AND SUNDAY

Straddling the bottom of a hill, this neighborhood recreation building leaves the best parts of the site for playing fields. While maintaining a playful scale, the well-articulated structure creates a rather grand space within.

25

WOODSON HIGH SCHOOL
55th and Eads Street, N. E.
1972—McLeod, Ferrara & Ensign
HOURS: 9 A.M. TO 3 P.M., OPEN FOR TOURS

A break from the recent past, Woodson is Washington's first modern high-rise high school, a response to increasing needs and diminishing sites.

R Maryland Places

Since 1846, when Alexandria, including that area now known as Arlington County, was ceded back to the State of Virginia, all of the District of Columbia, about sixty-eight square miles, has lain within the original boundaries of the State of Maryland. Maryland, which had its beginnings in 1634, was fairly well populated by 1791 when the Federal City was established; many of the early landowners, such as the Carroll, Peter, Digges and Addison families, were important in the city's formation and early history. For a long time the counties just outside the ten-mile square, Montgomery and Prince Georges, retained their rural character; they were important agricultural areas, and Washington families retired for the summer to rusticate in happy isolation less than fifteen miles from the zero milestone.

In this century, however, these areas have changed radically. The old county seats of Upper Marlboro (1706) and Rockville (1776) continue to grow, but suburban development has spread at an accelerated pace; country crossroads like Silver Spring, Bethesda, Wheaton and Hyattsville have become formless urban centers on the outskirts of Washington. Yet, prosperous farms and orchards still flourish in the outer reaches of the counties, and one can still find some of the old manor houses, carefully restored and treasured by their owners.

FOREST GLEN
(National Park Seminary)
Forest Glen, Maryland
1887—T. F. Schneider (Ye Forest Inne)

Originally the site of a country resort hotel, the center-piece of a promotional land-development scheme, the Inn was acquired in 1894 by John Irving Cassedy, who founded a finishing school for girls, the National Park Seminary. Thereafter, for a period of more than thirty years, a collection of strange and romantic buildings were constructed, including sorority houses in the form of a Japanese pagoda, a Dutch windmill, a Swiss chalet, an Indian Mission, an English castle and in other exotic styles. Since 1942, when the school was acquired by the Army, it has been an annex of the Walter Reed Medical Center. Plans for preservation and a new adaptive use of the buildings and site are now under study by the Maryland–National Capital Park and Planning Commission.

GREENBELT
Greenbelt, Maryland
1936—Clarence Stein, Hale Walker

A government development for low-income families, with construction work done by men taken from relief rolls. Such amenities as limited road access, a small lake, and special play areas for children were harbingers of future private developments.

3

COLUMBIA, MARYLAND
1964—The Rouse Company
James W. Rouse, William E. Finley, Wallace
Hamilton, Morton Hoppenfeld, planners

Columbia, Maryland, one of the two most publicized New Towns within the Washington, D.C. region, is even more closely related to the Baltimore metropolitan area. Better known for its planning innovations and intentions than for architectural consistency or excellence, Columbia has developed steadily as a community with a wide range of housing choices (in the moderate and upper-moderate range), commercial, recreational, educational and employment centers.

4

CONDON RESIDENCE
6805 Georgia Street
Chevy Chase, Maryland
1966—David H. Condon
Private residence

A classic example of a new residence upon a small lot within an established neighborhood, this contemporary dwelling shows a sensitive design response to existing conditions. Presenting a somewhat formal and reserved single-story facade to the street, the shed roof rises to two stories in the rear which open on a sheltered and enclosed garden court.

5

PHILLIPS-BREWER HOUSE
7705 Connecticut Avenue
Chevy Chase, Maryland
1968—Hartman-Cox
Private residence

Sited at one corner of a major intersection, this residence stakes out its own environment by turning its back to the street gaining access, instead, from an alley cul-de-sac, and including within the protection of its volume three exterior courtyards and interior accommodation for several generations of a single family. Relationship to the scale and silhouette of neo-Colonial neighbors is reflected in the broken massing and angles of plan and elevation. The results are clearly a case history of how a small corner lot, bypassed by developers and considered unbuildable, may, in skilled hands, be turned into an opportunity to achieve architectural distinction.

HAYES MANOR
4101 Manor Road
Chevy Chase, Maryland
1767—Alexander Williamson

One of Maryland's genuine Georgian houses, which stands today surrounded by the suburban excrescence of the past fifty years. Reverend Williamson originally purchased 700 acres, half of the tract known as "Clean Drinking Water," on which he built the central portion of the residence. Since 1792, it has been the seat of six generations of the Dunlop family, who constructed the wings in the nineteenth and twentieth centuries.

CEDAR LANE UNITARIAN CHURCH
9601 Cedar Lane
Bethesda, Maryland
1960, 1968—Keyes, Lethbridge & Condon
**   Pietro Belluschi, Associate Architect**
Visitors welcome

Of the three phases designated in the original master plan, the first, a Sunday school and auditorium (1960), and second, a chapel (1968), are complete. The third phase, a major space for worship, will, when constructed, enclose the existing courtyard on three sides. Careful siting, natural landscaping and simple materials used to advantage in a residential scale all contribute to make this complex a welcome neighbor.

8

BETHESDA NAVAL HOSPITAL
Wisconsin Avenue
Bethesda, Maryland
1940—Frederick Southwick, Chief Architect for the Navy
Paul Cret, Consulting Architect

A medical school, hospital, dental school and research center are incorporated in the tower and its wings.

9

GOVERNMENT EMPLOYEES INSURANCE COMPANY
Wisconsin and Western Avenues
Bethesda, Maryland
1959—Vincent Kling

Thoughtful siting, combined with a clear articulation of individual bays and elements, successfully breaks down the scale and mitigates much of the industrial atmosphere of this large complex. The consistent juxtaposition of long, low fenestrated wings agains higher opaque blocks not only expresses the plan within but also permits flexibility in siting and expansion.

10

MILTON
(Nathan Loughboro house)
5312 Allendale Road
Bethesda, Maryland
c. 1700 — East wing
c. 1808 — Main house — Nathan Loughboro, owner-builder
c. 1844 — West wing

It is believed that the east wing of this old stone house was built as a Dutch-Indian trading post at the beginning of the eighteenth century, which would make it the oldest surviving structure in the Washington area by a considerable margin.

11

RIVER ROAD UNITARIAN CHURCH
6301 River Road
Bethesda, Maryland
1965 — Keyes, Lethbridge & Condon
Visitors welcome

This serene building for worship displays, inside and out, a remarkably bold and consistently appropriate use of natural wood and painted brick in both theme and variation, completely clothing the shell which is, itself, a direct expression of the manipulation of interior space and light. The wooded character of the site has been preserved by the grading of drives and parking bays, an instance where trees clearly held precedence over cars.

12

POTOMAC OVERLOOK
Mohican Drive and MacArthur Boulevard
Glen Echo, Maryland
1956–59—Keyes, Lethbridge and Condon

This development is in a wooded gorge above the Potomac which had previously been passed over as undevelopable. Its success in turning the site to great scenic advantage and the unity of architecture and site attained shows the lack of imagination of the original negative assumption.

13

CABIN JOHN AQUEDUCT BRIDGE
Cabin John, Maryland
1859—Montgomery C. Meigs, engineer-designer

Washington's counterpart of the Pont du Gard, this bold engineering masterpiece carries the city's principal water supply, and a 20-foot road, across the Cabin John Creek, 100 feet above the valley floor. Until this century its 220-foot span was the largest single masonry arch in the world.

14

BANNOCKBURN COOPERATIVE HOUSES
Wilson Lane at McArthur Blvd.
1949—Vernon de Mars, Rhees Burket, Joseph Neufeld

Part of a pioneer postwar cooperative housing project, this first group of detached houses was constructed before financial, zoning and management problems undermined the enterprise.

15

KRIEGER-JACKSON HOUSE
Brigadoon Drive
Bethesda, Maryland
1959—Marcel Breuer

16

STANLEY TEMPCHIN HOUSE
7001 Crail Drive
1967—Charles W. Moore

17

CARDEROCK SPRINGS COMMUNITY
River Road
Bethesda, Maryland
1960–1968 — Keyes, Lethbridge & Condon
Visitors welcome (except to private residences)

This community is one of the early suburban residential developments to make use of cluster planning, with groups of three or four dwellings on a cul-de-sac and drives set back from feeder roadways. Neighborhood recreation facilities within safe and easy walking distance are provided by a community center sited on the edge of a regional park bordering the community on the southeast.

18

ROBERT L. WRIGHT HOUSE
7927 Deepwell Drive
Bethesda, Maryland
1958 — Frank Lloyd Wright

This house is designed entirely in segments of circles. It is one of a series based on circular forms.

19

KEYS HOUSE
River Road
Potomac, Maryland
1960 — Arthur H. Keyes, Jr.

On the uphill side, house and out-buildings enclose a sheltered entrance court. On the river side, cantilevers reach out over the hill to magnificent views up and down the Potomac.

20

GREAT FALLS OF THE POTOMAC
Park Service Inn
Great Falls, Maryland

The 50-foot waterfall dashes down between wild, dark rocks, and over and around gargantuan boulders in an intricate system of channels, cataracts, rapids and white-water stretches. On the Maryland side, a popular diversion is to scramble up and down on the rocks to view the falls from below, or to stroll beside the quiet shaded waters of the canal.

21

FORT WASHINGTON
1808
1815—Reconstructed by L'Enfant, Armistead

The site of this little-known or -appreciated fort was picked by Washington himself for its strategic value. It affords as a dividend a full scenic panorama both up and down the Potomac. This romantic shambles has been abandoned by the Army and is now being restored by the Park Service.

MOUNT VERNON

Washington is at the southern edge of the "fall line," which is a stretch about ten miles wide, where the waters from the Piedmont Plateau tumble down to the Coastal Plain. The Virginia environs of Washington reflect this change; and they produce, within a relatively limited space, interesting contrasts of topography, soil, and foliage. This area also provides the observer with a splendid opportunity to compare the architecture of a rich past with modern methods, materials, and forms, as well as to enjoy the pleasure of recognition when past and present share some measure of continuity and excellence.

DULLES INTERNATIONAL AIRPORT
Chantilly, Virginia
1962—Eero Saarinen & Associates

*". . . the new jet airport for our nation's capital also
should convey its purpose by its architectural expression.
The excitement of travel and the stateliness of belonging
to the federal capital should be conveyed."*
—Eero Saarinen, Perspecta 7

This is Washington's jet airport for the future, rather than
the present. It is significant and, more often than not,
revolutionary on all levels: as structure and architecture,
as a transportation machine, and as town planning. Of
particular interest are the hammock-like suspension roof,
multilevel circulation, and the mobile lounges.

2

RESTON, VIRGINIA
1973—Robert E. Simon
     Whittlesey and Conklin, planners
Visitors welcome

Nationally recognized for its premier effort in contemporary New Town planning, Reston was conceived as a unique private real estate venture which would, at one stroke, integrate residences, industry, commerce, schools, religious and cultural institutions into a satellite city—ideal for butcher, baker, banker and GS-15 civil servant. Architecturally this promise was fulfilled in the varied early examples of work by Whittlesey and Conklin, Charles M. Goodman, Chloethiel W. Smith and others. More recently, since the advent of management by Gulf-Reston, the range of architectural choice and quality has varied. The community has grown from a 1965 resident population of 500 to approximately 20,000 in 1972.

SCOPE BUILDING
Reston Industrial Park
1967—Jansons, Roberts, Taylor Associates

LAKE ANNE NURSERY KINDERGARTEN
1972—Kamstra, Abrash, Dickerson Associates

3

COLVIN RUN MILL
Route 7, Great Falls, Virginia
1973 Restoration—Fairfax County Park Authority
Visitors welcome

This early example of the functional tradition (first documentary evidence of a mill at this site occurs in 1811) illustrates completely the difficulties and triumphs inherent in accurate historic restoration. It is also a testament to the determination of a public body to employ continual and painstaking effort in the service of complete authenticity. As installed in the Grist Mill at Colvin Run, Oliver Evans' revolutionary milling technique (1794) is one of the earliest recorded perfected forms of automation. The simplicity of the foursquare masonry housing belies the complexity within, encompassing carefully reproduced pre-industrial machinery, bygone methods and materials, and the life-styles and setting for but one (1810) significant segment selected from Colvin Mill's long and varied local history.

4

WOLF TRAP FARM PARK
Vienna, Virginia
1971—MacFadyen & Knowles
Visitors welcome

An outdoor pavilion for the performing arts seating 3500 people under roof and an additional 4000 on adjacent lawns, Wolf Trap Theatre, a wood shelter of robust and dramatic form, has become the most popular summer mecca of its type in the metropolitan Washington area.

5

GREAT FALLS VISITORS CENTER
Great Falls, Virginia
1968—Kent Cooper & Associates
Visitors welcome

Exhibit space, auditorium and National Park Service Orientation Center are here elevated above the level of the occasional flood waters of the Potomac River. This response to site conditions led to a use of gradual access ramps which in form recall the locks of the nearby ruins of the historic Potomack Barge Canal.

6

MADEIRA SCHOOL
Greenway, Fairfax County, Virginia
1930—Waldron Faulkner, original quadrangles and campus
1970—David N. Yerkes and Associates, theater and
      student building
Private School

The wooded site and domestic scale of the earlier Georgian Revival buildings give the campus an intimate residential character.

Of the more recent buildings, carried out in the same range of materials, the Theater is outstanding for its skillful planning and massing—and for the views of the Potomac gorge seen from its interior lounges.

HARVEY RESIDENCE
8639 Overlook Road
McLean, Virginia
1972—Hugh Newell Jacobsen
Private residence

The steep shed roofs and frame turrets of this cypress-clothed dwelling seem to evoke a medieval concern for clerestory light. Extensive use of glass in walls, panels, unexpected slits and angled oriels permits the interior space to enjoy a remarkably constant quality of reflected light, lending further emphasis to its spare elegance.

CABOT HOUSE
Route #2—Bullsneck Hundred
McLean, Virginia
1958—Charles M. Goodman
Private residence

This contemporary ark perched on its riverside Ararat exploits superb scenery up and down river from almost every room. Basically a cypress-sided steel cage, the interior spaces are arranged about a central court, a welcome reference to human scale.

9

**BRICK INSTITUTE OF AMERICA
HEADQUARTERS BUILDING
1750 Old Meadow Road
McLean, Virginia
1968—Charles M. Goodman Associates
Private offices**

In terms of sheer mass and sensuous fluid use of brick, which sheathes (and funded) this association headquarters and research laboratory, and despite a weighted base here turned upside down, one is curiously reminded of the much more imposingly scaled triumph of the French Gothic, Albi Cathedral. Though the BIA building receives only a fleeting inspection from Route 495 Beltway, this all-brick, load-bearing structure immediately conveys an appropriate and impressive image of the material's design and structural versatility.

10

**PINE SPRING DEVELOPMENT HOUSES
Route #50
Fairfax County, Virginia
1952—Keyes, Smith, Satterlee & Lethbridge**

Here garden apartments serve as a buffer between the highway and the houses. Built all at once, the development utilized mass on-site prefabrication. Although there are but two basic house types, they have been skillfully modified to give the impression of a greater number of designs.

FOUNTAIN OF FAITH
National Memorial Park
Route 29-211, West of
Falls Church, Virginia
1952—Carl Milles, sculptor
Visitors welcome

The fountain, filled with bronze figures by the famous Swedish sculptor, is one of the most notable works of contemporary art in the Washington area. Another heroic figure by Milles overlooks the cemetery from a nearby knoll. The Monument to Four Chaplains, a World War II memorial by Constantino Nivola, is also worthy of special notice.

FALLS CHURCH EPISCOPAL
115 E. Fairfax St.
Falls Church, Virginia
c. 1767—James Wren
Visitors welcome

The present Georgian brick church, located on the site of a previous frame structure (1734), was designed and guided through construction by the same architect responsible for Christ Church, Alexandria, which employed a similar plan with galleries. Renovations occured in 1830, 1866, 1906 and most extensively in 1969 when the interior was restored to its "original" character (including actual construction of the Wren gallery) for the first time since its occupation and looting by Northern troops during the War between the States.

13

GLEBE HOUSE
4527 17th Street
Arlington, Virginia
1775
1850 (octagon addition)
Private residence

Patented originally as "glebe lands" (rectory with farm for maintenance of the clergy) to serve Fairfax Parish which included Christ Church, Alexandria and Falls Church, Glebe House was rescued from confiscation at the time of the Commonwealth's dissolution of church property in 1802 by the adroit legal defense of Edmund Jennings Lee. Partially burned in 1808, (the entire glebe was sold in 1815 to the benefit of the Parish) the cottage was rebuilt in 1820 using the original walls and foundations. The octagon wing is most likely the studio additon of sculptor Clark Mills (the equestrian Jackson in Lafayette Square, the equestrian Washington in the Circle of the same name).

14

UNITARIAN CHURCH OF ARLINGTON
4444 Arlington Boulevard
Arlington, Virginia
1964—Charles M. Goodman Associates

This is but one of several significant new Unitarian churches in the Washington area. It is perhaps the least traditional in structure and form.

15

NAVY AND MARINE MEMORIAL
Mt. Vernon Memorial Highway at Boundry Channel Inlet
Arlington, Virginia
1941—H. W. Corbett, architect
1930—Ernesto Begni Del Piatta, sculptor
Visitors welcome

Breakers and wheeling birds frozen in bronze-finished aluminum crest a green granite ground swell, which is clearly late W.P.A.

16

GOODMAN HOUSE
514 North Quaker Lane
Alexandria, Virginia
1958—Charles M. Goodman Associates
Private residence

The nucleus of structure here, a two-story, turn-of-the-century farmhouse, gutted and rebuilt, its spaces opened up, has received an elegantly detailed single-story frame and glass wing. A seven-acre site, fencing and plantings insure privacy and a favorable elevation on the west escarpment of the Potomac overlooking Alexandria guarantees a panoramic view of the river valley below the Fall Line.

17

SEVAREID-SYME HOUSE
1226 North Pegram Street
Alexandria, Virginia
1941—Charles M. Goodman Associates

At the remove of more than a quarter of a century, the simplicity and clarity of this statement remain an unqualified success and bear comparison with more recent experimentation.

18

THE VIRGINIA THEOLOGICAL SEMINARY
Bohlen, Aspinwall & Meade Halls
Seminary Hill
Alexandria, Virginia
1859–1861—Starkweather and Plowman
Private buildings for education

Constructed on the site of the original Seminary Hall (1832–1835), this somewhat tenuously knitted brick trio with gothicized masonry relief enjoys, excepting the summit cross, something of the no-nonsense aggressive confidence of a mid-nineteenth-century, Southern military school. Such an air is due, perhaps to a limited budget and to the pressing need for space caused by the rapid growth of the Seminary in the years prior to the War between the States. Such is also due in the extreme to the recent removal of counterpositioned frame bay windows and porticoes from Bohlen (left) and Meade (right) Halls and by the loss of a broad one-story gallery which marched across the front of Aspinwall (center) Hall, tying the three together. Upon the authority of an 1856 edition of *The Southern Churchman*, "the style of architecture of Aspinwall Hall is 'Elizabethan,'" and considered very "beautiful and imposing."

HOLLIN HILLS (Original group)
Fort Hunt Road
Alexandria, Virginia
1948–54—Charles M. Goodman Associates

The first major architect-designed community of detached houses in the area, this is an outstanding example of a long-range and sustained program of land acquisition and development. Only a few houses were built at any one time.

It is no less significant for the quality and variety as well as for the careful placement of the buildings that exploit the natural amenities of this suburban site.

MOUNT VERNON
Terminal, Mount Vernon Memorial Highway
Mount Vernon, Virginia
1751–1761 George Washington
Walter Macomber (architect for restoration)
Visitors welcome

Mount Vernon is first and foremost an intimate biography of the intelligence, energy, taste and warmth of its owner-architect, George Washington. These qualities of Washington are everywhere evident, and the precise and elegant restoration done in this century on the house, out-buildings and plantation is an appropriate tribute from a grateful nation.

21

WOODLAWN PLANTATION
U.S. #1, 7.8 miles south of Alexandria
Mount Vernon, Virginia
1800–05 — Dr. William Thornton
Visitors welcome

Here Thornton's efforts have provided a standard for domestic architecture throughout Virginia. The 2000-acre estate once part of Mount Vernon was Washington's wedding gift to Major Lawrence Lewis, his nephew and Nellie Custis, Lewis's wife (Martha Washington's granddaughter), in the days when familial affections were solidly expressed.

22

POPE-LEIGHY HOUSE
Woodlawn Plantation
U.S. #1
Mount Vernon, Virginia
1940 — Frank Lloyd Wright
(Built in Falls Church, Virginia;
moved to present location, 1964.)

One of Wright's "Usonian" series for clients with modest means.

23

POHICK CHURCH
U.S. #1, 12 miles south of Alexandria
Fairfax County, Virginia
1769–74—George Washington
Visitors welcome

James Wren's design for Christ Church, Alexandria, was evidently Washington's model. The quoined corners and pedimented doors, flanked by Ionic pilasters, all of Aquia stone, provide the only relief for the decidedly handsome and severe Flemish bond elevations. The Vestry House (1931), opposite, admirably complements this building.

24

GUNSTON HALL
4 miles east of U.S. #1 on Virginia #242
Lorton, Virginia
1758—William Buckland
Visitors welcome

It is well to be reminded that George Mason, the original owner of Gunston Hall, authored one of the most important statements on human rights in the history of Western civilization:

"That all men are created equally free and independent and have certain inherent natural Rights . . . among which are the Enjoyment of Life and Liberty, with the means of acquiring and possessing Property, and pursuing and obtaining Happiness and Safety."

The first view of this simple, low-massed brick Georgian residence, its flanking dependencies now vanished, gives no hint of the superb distinction of its interior spaces, nor of the boxwood allee and sunken garden beyond.

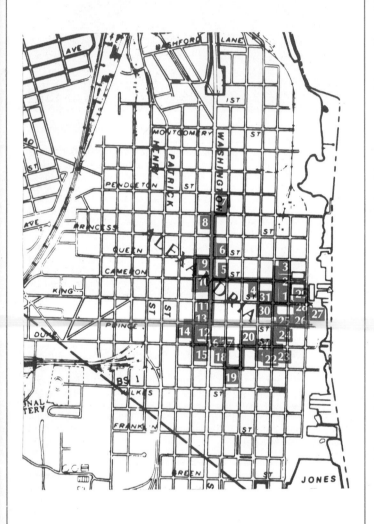

In 1732, at the foot of what is now Oronoco Street, a warehouse (terminal for the "rolling road" which brought hogsheads of tobacco from the inland plantations) was constructed at a location on the riverbank where a ferry some years before had been established to carry the Kings Highway across the Potomac to Maryland. In 1742, when Fairfax County was formed from Prince William County, a nucleus of businesses and residences had developed about this central "warehouse," and in 1748, by act of the General Assembly, Alexandria formally came into being, named for the Alexander family, owners of the town site. On July 13, 1749, a board of trustees was set, a municipal government organized, and thirty-one of its gridded half-acre lots surveyed by Colonel John West, Jr., assisted by George Washington, were sold. Heir to a splendid natural harbor serving a vast agricultural hinterland, and situated athwart the major road running from Charleston to Boston, Alexandria rapidly became one of the early Republic's most important port cities.

Completion of the railroad from the Ohio River Valley to Baltimore in the eighteen-forties and the rise of fast and relatively efficient clipper-ship service from that city eventually offered strenuous competition to Alexandria's shipping. Because it was occupied by Northern troops at the beginning of the War between the States, Alexandria was spared the physical ravages typical of that conflict but it shared with Virginia and the rest of the South the general poverty of the postwar period. Principally due to such economic determinants during the nineteenth century, Alexandria, like Charleston, was able (without benefit of Gothic Revival aculturation) to preserve into this century a significantly large inventory of mid-Georgian and Federal domestic architecture. The city's current prosperity, dating from 1932 with the rapid growth of the Federal Government and discovery of the convenience of old Alexandria to the nearby Federal City, has stimulated extensive architectural restoration and renovation.

RAMSAY HOUSE
N.E. corner King & Fairfax Streets
c. 1725, restored 1956
Visitors welcome

Undeniable gambreled charm and stepped garden entrance enhance this residence, which, according to local tradition, was moved by barge from Dumfries, Virginia, in 1749 by William Ramsay, Alexandria's first citizen and its first and only Lord Mayor.

CARLYLE HOUSE
121 N. Fairfax Street
1752—John Ariss, attribution
1974—J. Everette Fauber, Jr., restoration
The North Virginia Regional Park Authority
To be opened to the public in 1976

This great mid-Georgian residence and its gardens are, at last, undergoing extensive restoration. Built for one of Alexandria's early and prominent merchants, Colonel John Carlyle, this dwelling has figured importantly in the city's and nation's history.

Also currently under restoration at the southeast corner of N. Fairfax and Cameron Streets is the Bank of Alexandria building (1803), a significant local example of commercial architecture of the early Federal Period.

3

THOMPSON-MARSHBURN HOUSE
211 N. Fairfax St.
1799–1817
Private apartments

Jonah Thompson, "shipping merchant, banker and large property owner" and prominent Alexandrian, constructed this double, or "married" house in an as yet unresolved sequence between 1799 and 1817. It is most probable that the building fronting the street with its handsome arched stone entrances, slender water table and immediacy to the public sidewalk originally served as his bank, business offices, and/or residence. It is, however, the structure attached at the rear, facing the Potomac River, with its truly remarkable Adam-style loggia of a grace not found elsewhere in Alexandria, that is a continuing source of mystery, for in all documentary evidence the two buildings are treated as one.

4

GADSBY'S
(City Tavern and City Hotel)
S.W. corner N. Royal and Cameron Streets
1752—City Tavern (smaller two-story building)
1792—John Wise—City Hotel
1974—J. Everette Fauber, Jr., restoration

Simplicity and attention to architectural detail mark Gadsby's, a most extraordinary "ordinary" of early America. For forty-seven years these buildings provided the public setting for many decisive events in George Washington's life, and today they still preside over the community life of Alexandria.

5

YEATON-FAIRFAX HOUSE
607 Cameron Street
1799–1807 — William Yeaton
A private residence

A stately town residence provided with Adam-cum-Federal details delicately improvised in the indigenous tradition.

Note the residences at 609 and 611 Cameron adjoining: most excellent and agreeable neighbors.

6

BROCKETT'S ROW
301–307 North Washington Street
c. 1840 — Robert Brockett
Private residences

"On the east side [of Washington Street] north of Queen Street a row of shabby frame houses sheltered the lowest class of Irish, whose drunken dances and 'wakes' kept a turmoil in the neighborhood until . . . Robert Brockett eradicated the shabby row, and built a frame row of four houses of a better class, which were soon occupied by respectable people."

—Mary Powell, *History of Old Alexandria, Virginia*

Urban renewal circa 1840! Roof dormers here have given way to small windows set on the line of the third floor.

7

ROBERT E. LEE HOUSE AND HALLOWELL SCHOOL
607–609 Oronoco Street
c. 1795
Private residences

These chaste mid-Georgian elevations, with the sensibility and force of character of a Jane Austen heroine, impart a unique continuity to the street.

Note also the Fendall-John L. Lewis House at 614 across the way, which is more reminiscent of the Yankee Coast than Tidewater Virginia.

8

EDMUND JENNINGS LEE HOUSE
S.W. corner Oronoco and N. Washington Streets
c. 1800
Private residence

Sober and precise Georgian, with the requisiste Vitruvian virtues, this residence is another lesson in urban responsibility as it prepares for and then turns the corner of the block, defining, as well, the intersection of streets.

9

LLOYD HOUSE
S.W. corner Queen and North Washington Streets
c. 1793—John Wise
Private offices

Splendid Alexandria Merchants' Georgian, which must, through properly scaled elevations, be reunited with the building mass of the remainder of the block. Past, indicative; future, indefinite.

10

CHRIST CHURCH AND YARD
Corners Cameron, North Columbus and
North Washington Streets
1767–1773, Tower 1818—James Wren
Visitors welcome

A half-block of green and a four-square structure with quoined corners and a remarkably fine interior, this church is a way station in pursuit of the Virginia mystique. George Washington occupied pew No. 60; Robert E. Lee, No. 46.

Christ Church invites comparison with three other churches in Northern Virginia, all built at approximately the same time: Falls Church (1767), Pohick Church (1769), and Aquia Church (1757).

WASHINGTON STREET METHODIST CHURCH
109 South Washington Street
1830
1875, present elevation
1899, present interior
Visitors welcome

Reconstruction Gothic shelters a congregation which has been always noted for forceful community leadership.

THE LYCEUM
S.W. corner Prince and South Washington Streets
1839–1858
1974—Carrol C. Curtice, restoration
City of Alexandria Visitors' Center
Open to the public

A haunting, unmistakable beauty typifies this classic example of the Greek Revival in America. Perhaps first among local buildings in the hearts of Alexandrians, restoration has at last halted the years of unconscionable neglect, and new civic use insures the Lyceum's lovely existence into an active future.

13

WILLIAM FOWLE HOUSE
711 Prince Street
Nucleus c. 1800 — William Fowle
Private residence

The setback from the property line and the entrance portico and doorway of this tree-shaded residence confirm a New England precedent. Its owner-builder came to Alexandria from Marblehead, Massachusetts. The materials and handling are local and notably successful.

14

THE CONFEDERATE MUSEUM
("Parson" Johnston House)
806 Prince Street
c. 1850
Open upon request. Contact Custodian, 548–6388.

The crisp brownstone lintels, ashlar coursing at sidewalk, and filigree balcony rail somewhat relieve the somber countenance of this mid-century Janus.

15

ST. JOHN'S ACADEMY
S.E. corner Duke and South Columbus Streets
c. 1833
Private apartments

"The special adaptation of Alexandria for schools, on account of its accessibility to many railroad connections; its proximity to the seat of Federal Government, giving easy access to its museums, art galleries, etc., without exposure to its allurements and temptations; the moral and religious character of our Alexandria community; the healthfulness of the city; its most excellent and pure water, give to this town a decided advantage over others . . ." (Advertisement for St. John's Academy).
—Brockett, *A Concise History of Alexandria, 1883*

16

LLOYD'S ROW
220–228 South Washington Street
621 Duke Street
1811–1816
Private residences

A family reunion for a united stand against urban erosion is mandatory for this handsome Federal townhouse group which originally included three two-story buildings (only one, much altered, now remains) along with the five three-story residences in existence. Noteworthy is the proportion of window opening to solid wall, a lesson obviously ignored by several newly reproduced neighbors.

THE DULANEY HOUSE
N.E. corner Duke (601) and South St. Asaph Streets
c. 1785
Private residence

This dwelling and its garden are an honored and elegant exercise in urban understatement.

THE LAWRASON-LAFAYETTE HOUSE
S.W. corner Duke and South St. Asaph Streets
c. 1820
Private residence

A justifiably celebrated and distinguished American Federal mansion.

19

VOWELL-SMITH HOUSE
S.E. corner Wolfe and South St. Asaph Streets
c. 1840
Private residence

This splendid villa is a valued landmark of the early transition of Federal into Gothic Revival. It still commands its original quarter of a city block, and remains one of Alexandria's few surviving examples of mid-nineteenth century eclectic vigor.

20

ST. PAUL'S EPISCOPAL CHURCH
N.E. corner Duke and South Pitt Streets
1817—Benjamin Henry Latrobe
1957—Delos Smith
1968—Adler, Rosenthal Architects, interior restoration
Visitors welcome

"What a confession of ostentatious poverty! The congregation are proud enough to build a handsome front to show the passengers, but too poor to be consistent in the flanks . . ."—Latrobe's comment to the Reverend William Wilmer in August 1817, upon the advice of his agent that the original design had been altered.

Delos Smith's additions are a vindication.

ST. MARY'S CATHOLIC CHURCH
E. side, 300 block, South Royal Street
1826—Original portion
Visitors welcome

Late 19th Century Gothic ecclesiology in substantial granite.

At 316 South Royal, the manse of the old Presbyterian Meeting House. Enter at right of the "Flounder" and walk through to graveyard and Meeting House.

PRESBYTERIAN MEETING HOUSE
W. side, 300 block, South Fairfax Street
1774
1836
Visitors welcome

A place of worship for the early Scots of Alexandria, appropriately expressed with gravity and clarity.

23

DR. JAMES CRAIK HOUSE
210 Duke Street
1789–1795
Private residence

A house as renowned for the handsome and plain-speaking truth of its mid-Georgian elevation as for its early owner, an eminent physician of Alexandria, whom George Washington styles in his will as "my compatriot in arms and old and intimate friend."

24

DR. WILLIAM BROWN HOUSE
212 South Fairfax Street
c. 1775
Private residence

Frame covers brick nogging in this most comfortable and agreeable Colonial town dwelling.

25

200 BLOCK PRINCE STREET
Mid-late 18th century

Perfectly scaled and subtly detailed building elevations contain and enrich the exterior space of the street, providing the city's most characteristic and complete architectural statement of the Alexandria mid-Georgian style. All are private residences except the Greek Revival "Athenaeum" at the Northwest corner of Prince and South Lee Streets, sheltering the Northern Virginia Fine Arts Association, to which visitors are welcome.

26

CAPTAINS' ROW
100 Block Prince Street
Late 18th, early 19th century

A complete environment proving that a whole may indeed exceed the sum of its part.

COL. JOHN FITZGERALD'S WAREHOUSE
S.E. corner King and Union Streets
c. 1765

Neither inadequate and unimaginative conversion to present use, nor thoughtless graphics can obscure the worth of this venerable building.

THE CORN EXCHANGE
S.W. corner King and Union Streets
1871
Private offices

A small, classically ordered red-brick Renaissance palazzo with rustic coursing, articulated pilasters, and bold cornice, which proclaim spittoons, bowlers, watch-chains, and cigars.

THE WAREHOUSES
N. side, 100 Block King Street
c. 1800

Unerring examples of the Functional Tradition, largely unrestored, this group of structures must be allowed to pass into a useful future with simplicity and dignity.

30

STABLER-LEADBEATER APOTHECARY SHOP
105–107 South Fairfax Street
1792—Restored, 1939
Visitors welcome

The lower elevation suggests a smart shop on Regent Street by Nash, which fails, however, to daunt the integrity of the Alexandria-Federal plain style above.

31

MARKET SQUARE
King at N. Royal & N. Fairfax Streets
1749
1967—Neer & Graef
Visitors welcome

Alexandria's central public space from its founding, this ground was used for fairs and political assemblies as well as the city's marketplace. Here George Washington drilled the Virginia Rangers (later the Virginia Militia) both before and after Braddock's ill-fated French campaign in 1755. In the nineteenth century the square became filled with residences, commercial structures and warehouses, the market having retreated to the courtyard of City Hall. Clearance and re-establishment of the square for public use has been part of the City's renewal of King Street, which, beginning in the last decade, continues in progress.

INDEX

A GUIDE TO THE ARCHITECTURE OF WASHINGTON, D.C.

Second Edition, Revised and Expanded

**Written and edited by Warren J. Cox,
Hugh Newell Jacobsen, Francis D. Lethbridge,
and David R. Rosenthal for the
Washington Metropolitan Chapter
of the American Institute of Architects**

*"The grandeur, the simplicity, and the beauty...
will, I doubt not, give it a preference in your
eyes as it has in mine."*

Thus George Washington, describing the proposed Capitol building, defined the high standards that to this day are met in the architecture of Washington, D.C. From the early Federal-style mansions and municipal buildings to the Washington Monument, from Dulles International Airport to a 552-acre urban-renewal complex—both the old and the new in the city reflect President Washington's original vision.

This fully illustrated working guide to the architecture of the greater Washington area is designed to aid the tourist as well as the professional architect—indeed, everyone interested in our nation's capital—discover this majestic city's best and most representative structures. Arranged into convenient walking and motoring tours, the book is a pictorial history that crosses the city and the centuries, leading the visitor down streets first planned by Pierre L'Enfant in 1791, into buildings designed by the finest architects of yesterday and today.

**McGraw-Hill Book Company
1221 Avenue of the Americas,
New York, N.Y. 10020**

07-013285-2